TALES FROM THE 2004-05 FIGHTING ILLINI

BRETT DAWSON

www.SportsPublishingLLC.com

ISBN: 1-59670-121-8

Publishers: Peter L. Bannon and Joseph J. Bannon Sr.
Senior managing editor: Susan M. Moyer
Acquisitions editor: Mike Pearson
Developmental editor: Doug Hoepker
Art director: K. Jeffrey Higgerson
Dust jacket design: Joseph Brumleve
Interior layout: Kathryn R. Holleman
Imaging: Kathryn R. Holleman, Dustin Hubbart
Photo editor: Erin Linden-Levy
Media and promotions managers: Mike Hagan (regional),
    Randy Fouts (national), Maurey Williamson (print)

Printed in the United States of America

Sports Publishing L.L.C.
804 North Neil Street
Champaign, IL 61820

Phone: 1-877-424-2665
Fax: 217-363-2073
www.SportsPublishingLLC.com

CONTENTS

FOREWORD
BY WAYNE McCLAIN
UNIVERSITY OF ILLINOIS ASSISTANT BASKETBALL COACH

In life, like in basketball, the difference between winning and losing is a matter of inches.

I grew up watching the Figthing Illini. I remember watching Bogie Redmon shoot hook shots for Illinois. And to come from that memory to the point where I was standing center stage with the University of Illinois for the biggest basketball game in school history—the 2005 NCAA championship game—it's one of the greatest feelings I'll ever have. When it's happening, you don't get time to think about it. When it's over, you almost want to pinch yourself.

But I could have easily been somewhere else. I could have left in 2001, when Bill Self did. I thought I was going to, in fact. I left my office one night thinking that I was leaving. The next day, I realized I was staying home.

You hear people talk about the basketball gods, well I think they smiled on me. Staying at Illinois was a huge gamble on my part. I didn't know who was going to come in to be the next coach. I didn't know if they would like me. A guy can come in and coach for a year and tell you in the end, "You're just not my type."

But I'm glad I stayed. And I'm indebted to Bruce Weber for letting me have the opportunity. I feel blessed that I was able to get in with our team in 2004-05 and enjoy the ride, as if I was in the movie *Driving Mr. Daisy*. I was able to climb in the back seat and ride around with a group of guys who showed me the world, and I just got to enjoy it. It was a great ride.

I've been around great teams before, winning three straight state championships at Peoria Manual High School. And when you think about great teams, work ethic is the common thread, and our guys were there every day. No excuses. There was never, "I'm sick, I'm tired." None of that.

The other thing this team displayed is a willingness to sacrifice for the greater good of the team. Jack Ingram and Nick Smith could have been major players on a lot of other teams. Roger Powell Jr. sacrificed a lot for our team. Dee Brown could've been our leading scorer. Instead, he was our leading scorer one game and our leading assist guy the next. Deron Williams was the same way. Luther Head guarded the other team's best player every night. James Augustine was a versatile guy who could do a lot of things, and we had to beg him to try to score. He was just that unselfish. All of them were that way. When you have guys who just don't give a dang who gets the glory or who's in the headlines—guys whose attitude is, "just win, baby"—that's when you've got something special.

When I look back at the 2004-05 season, the first thing that I'll remember is our team's competitiveness. They were a group of guys that each had a strong drive, a great work ethic. They made each other better every day. But I'll also remember the what-ifs: The Ohio State game, and how close that was, how we were in control and let it get away; The North Carolina game when we were at 70-70 and we were right there. You can look back and say that we could have had an even more special season—a season everyone would remember, not just people in Illinois. That lives in me every day.

I'll also remember our fans. Every day was like traveling with a band. It was like being with a rock star. I've seen on MTV the way those guys live, the fame that they experience, and I think for a year, we lived that. We snuck in and out of hotels, we had special ways to get into arenas. We had to barricade off paths to get to our bus because everybody wanted to get to our guys. It was incredible. Those were the benefits of the hard work, the early mornings, the weights, the late nights. Those guys were never bigger than life to me, because I saw them every day, but the outside perception was that they were larger than life.

I can't express in words what our fans meant to our team in 2004-05. I compare it to jogging in the heat. If you're alone and you have 200 more yards to go, you're going to quit. It's hot and you're tired, and you're going to want to stop. But if there are 25 friends and family members cheering for you, you're going to push on and finish. That's how it was with our team. I can remember like it was yesterday when Jack Ingram raised his hands coming out of a time-out during the Arizona game, and our fans responded. The noise, the life they gave us, it was like a breath of fresh air. They gave us that little bit of energy that we needed. On paper, the team won that game. But in our hearts, we know that a lot of the credit belongs to our fans.

A few months after the season ended, I was in Florida on a recruiting trip, and college coaches were still telling me that they enjoyed watching Illinois play. They told me that not only did they enjoy our success, but that they enjoyed the style of play, the way we shared the ball. I think that we raised the bar for a lot of teams.

We raised the bar for Illinois, too. You never want to go backward. We knocked on the door in 2004-05. The next time, we want to knock the door down. We know that it won't be easy. If you look at it realistically, you might never duplicate a season like that. North Carolina won the national championship, but they were one play away from losing in the Sweet 16 to Villanova. You can have the greatest team, the most talent in the nation, but if you don't get a few breaks, you might never experience that kind of magic again. We had that kind of magical season in 2004-05, and I know that I'll never forget it.

Over the years, I've collected some pictures that I keep in my office. Frank Williams hitting his big shot to beat Minnesota for a share of the Big Ten title. Luther Head making his putback against Purdue to clinch a share of the conference championship. Those memories are so dear to me. But from 2004-05, I don't have anything like that. I'll never wear a ring or a watch, I swear. I'll give every one of them away. And I don't have any pictures or keepsakes or mementos. I don't need them, because that season is embedded in me.

A team like the 2004-05 Fighting Illini lives on in your heart. It lives forever inside you.

INTRODUCTION

By Brett Dawson

At the moment of his greatest coaching triumph, Bruce Weber was at a loss for words. He had only tears—of joy and pain and sheer confusion—and a bewildered feeling in perfect keeping with the game he'd just coached. Illinois had defeated Arizona to advance to its first NCAA Final Four in 16 years, and Weber, the architect of perhaps the finest season in Illini basketball history, was humbled by the moment. Maybe, somehow, he knew there would never be another quite like it.

At 48, Weber had reached a professional peak that retiring coaches spend their careers dreaming of: reaching the Final Four. He had done it in the most improbable of ways, coaching a team that came within a three-pointer of achieving regular-season perfection, that had been dead and buried with four minutes to play in that Arizona game, only to stave off its season's end and win the most compelling game in exactly 100 years of Illinois basketball.

"I could coach the rest of my life and never have another year like [this]," Weber said. "You're aware of that. You certainly hope you put together teams to make runs in the tournament in the future, but this was something special. You dream about years like this."

That, more than anything else, was the tale of the 2004-05 Illinois basketball season. These Illini, from the beginning, seemed marked for greatness, destined to rewrite the hoop history of the school in Year 100. And though Illinois fell just short of its ultimate goal—removing its label as the best college basketball program never to win a national championship—it had a season that, by any measure, could be called nothing short of a smashing success.

"It's the kind of year you never forget," said guard Luther Head, and there could be no doubting that assessment. Over the course of 171 dizzying days, Weber would forge his veteran players into a cohesive team that proved almost unbeatable. In the end, it would take a North Carolina team blessed with four players who would be first-round selections in the NBA draft to derail the Illini express. And even then, Illinois did not go down without a fight.

The magic of 2004-05 extended well beyond the court. It spread across the Illinois campus, where players were stopped daily by classmates asking them to pose for photos or sign T-shirts. It extended to Chicago and Peoria and across the state of Illinois, a place hungry for a winner and quick to adopt a team that bought in completely to Weber's brand of unselfish, team-first basketball.

"People just really liked our team, and that made you feel good," Head said. "Anytime somebody shows you that kind of love and support, it's a great thing. I would go up to people on campus and just ask them to take a picture with me, just regular people I saw walking around, because I wanted them to know how good it felt."

It would be hard for anyone to understand. This was not a program—nor a collection of players, save perhaps Dee Brown—that had spent years in the spotlight. This was not Duke, the current flagship program in college basketball. It wasn't Kentucky or North Carolina, the bluebloods with the richest traditions and the most all-time wins in college basketball history. It wasn't even Kansas, the program that nurtured the game more than a century ago, and just two years prior had demonstrated its historical superiority by hiring away Illinois' coach, Bill Self.

This was Illinois, an always-solid program that came into its own in 2005, proving to be one of the game's greatest coming-of-age stories in the process.

"I think we were kind of new, and people liked that about us," Weber said. "Fans get tired of the same teams winning. Maybe the fact that we weren't Duke or Kentucky or Carolina or UCLA kind of drew people to us a little bit. That, and the way we played."

The way they played was something to see, all extra passes and extraordinary defense. In an era when so many pundits had mourned the state of college basketball, these Illini were at the center of the game's great resurgence. Years from now, we might look back at 2004-05 as the year that college basketball made a comeback. And Illinois' comeback kids might be more emblematic of that than any team in basketball. Anyone who saw them can appreciate the team's significance—not only to the school, but to the game.

I'm one of those people. I was there when the curtain went up on an early morning practice on October 15, 2004, and when the final horn sounded on North Carolina's 75-70 national championship victory April 4, 2005. Those dates seem like only yesterday, and in truth, we aren't so far removed from Illinois' best-ever basketball season. But the hope is that you'll enjoy this up-close perspective of the season, and that you'll learn a little something along the way, too.

And if nothing else, I hope you'll get something out of reminiscing about it all. It's a season worth remembering, after all. And, as Bruce Weber knows, it might be a long time before any of us sees another the likes of it.

THE HYPE

The calendar may say that the college basketball season begins in mid-October, but the season never seems to end in this sleepy little college town. One season blurs into the next, as basketball has become a year-round obsession in Champaign-Urbana. So although Bruce Weber guided his Illini through their first practice on a chilly October morning in 2004, Illinois' centennial basketball season had begun long before.

It's hard to pinpoint exactly when. In some ways, it was conceived four years earlier, when Bill Self, Weber's predecessor as the head coach at Illinois, had signed the core of the team as high school seniors. Dee Brown came on board first, then James Augustine and Deron Williams, the latter a pure point guard considered a coup in particular, because Self proved his recruiting reach could stretch to Texas. In other ways, it began on a snowy night in February of 2004, when, during a game at Indiana, the Illini rallied from a 12-point deficit for the galvanizing win first-year coach Weber had been seeking all season. It was for Weber a seminal moment, the night when he finally felt that he'd forged the players he inherited from Self into his own team that was capable of making a deep postseason run.

The Illini, though, might tell you that Weber's second season began the moment his first ended. In the moments after Illinois' 2004 season ended with a loss to Duke in the NCAA tournament's Sweet 16, Weber addressed his team in a locker room stunned to silence. And the coach delivered a message that would carry through the summer.

"All summer, everyone's going to be talking about how good we're going to be," Weber told his team. "You're going to hear about how we have everyone coming back and how high we're going to be ranked. But that's up to you."

Don't stagnate, Weber urged to his team. Take care of business, on the court and in the classroom. "He told us we couldn't just show up and be great—we had to earn it," Brown said. And the Illini set out to do just that.

Brown and Williams would tour the country taking part in camps built to expand on their considerable potential. At the Nike All-America Camp, they'd serve as counselors to the nation's best high school players at night, then rise early in the morning for heated pickup games against the best that college basketball had to offer. At Michael Jordan's camp in California, Brown and Williams would take another step forward, playing against topflight college and NBA players and even sharing the court with Jordan himself.

"I did pretty well against him," Williams said. "I was like, 'I'm hanging with Jordan right now.'"

While Brown and Williams were jet-setting, their teammates back home were working just as hard. Luther Head was perfecting an erratic jump shot, taking on Weber's challenge to become the best three-point shooter in the Big Ten. Roger Powell Jr., who had surprised his teammates by putting his name in the NBA draft after his junior season, learned he was unlikely to be drafted into the league, and thus returned over the summer hungry to fill the holes in his game. Augustine and senior Jack Ingram would visit big-man camps to hone their post play. And sophomores Warren Carter, Rich McBride, and Brian Randle would use their first full summer on campus to improve their physical conditioning as well as their basketball skill.

"There was a feeling that we could be really, really good," Carter said. "Nobody wanted to take that for granted."

It's hard to say when the 2004-05 basketball season began for Illinois. But on a sweltering July day at the Nike Camp in Indianapolis, it clearly was in full swing. Sitting on the metal bleachers at the National Institute for Fitness and Sport, newly hired Southern Illinois coach Chris Lowery—an assistant to Weber in his first season at Illinois—watched the best high school talent in America doing its best to impress a who's who of college coaches. Lowery had stayed in touch with Weber, and he had seen Brown and Williams at the camp counselor games that week. He was aware that Illinois had a season-long celebration planned to honor its 100th year of basketball. The stars were aligned, Lowery figured. Finally.

"You watch," he said leaning back against those metal bleachers. "That team is going to the Final Four."

Fever Pitch

Illinois fans entered 2004-05 starving for some success. The program had become a consistent Big Ten contender, winning or sharing the league title in four of the previous seven years. But NCAA tournament success had eluded Illinois. The school's last trip to the Final Four, the true barometer of college basketball greatness, had come in 1989, when Lou Henson's Flyin' Illini had marched to Seattle only to come up short in the national semifinal against bitter Big Ten rival Michigan.

When Weber was hired in the spring of 2003, he became the third coach to lead the program since Henson was forced out in 1996. Lon Kruger first took over for Henson and put the Illini back on the map, tapping the fertile recruiting ground in Peoria to reel in some of the most important recruits in school history, among them Frank Williams and Sergio McClain. Bill Self took over when Kruger bolted for the NBA's Atlanta Hawks, and he seemed poised to take the program to new heights. His first team whetted the appetite of Illinois fans, who fell in love with a hard-nosed bunch that put the "fight" in Fighting Illini. Illinois came up just short of the Final Four in 2001, losing a hard-fought game against Arizona.

When Self left for Kansas two years later, Weber inherited a team that had come up just shy of a Big Ten championship but had lost its heart in forward Brian Cook, drafted after his senior season in the first round by the Los Angeles Lakers. Illinois was talented and deep, but in Weber's mind not experienced enough to make a run at the national championship.

"The first day I met with them, I started talking about the Final Four in St. Louis," Weber said. "And they're all like, 'Coach, the Final Four is in San Antonio this year.'"

Weber had been looking a year ahead, to his second season, when he felt Illinois would be better equipped for a Final Four run. In hindsight, he said, it might have been a bad idea to share that thought with his team. But Weber was hardly the only one looking ahead to 2005. Illinois fans had circled the season since Brown and Williams were freshmen, and by October of 2004, fans were itching to get it started.

"The whole offseason, everybody was talking to us about 'Final Four this and Final Four that,'" Augustine said. "It was all you heard."

Adding to Illini nation's appetite were the bleak fortunes of its football team. After a 1-11 season in 2003, Ron Turner's team was struggling again in 2004, and on a cloudy afternoon in October, it was clear just how ready the Illini faithful had become for hoops. That day, Illinois lost 30-19 to Michigan at Memorial Stadium. Shortly thereafter, just across Kirby Avenue, the doors to the Assembly Hall opened, welcoming beleaguered fans to "Illini Basketball Madness," an afternoon variation on "Midnight Madness" that not only served to publicly tip off the season—it took place just a few hours after Illinois' first, private practice of the year—but to unveil the school's All-Century basketball team. As fans filed in, a wide-eyed high schooler named Chester Frazier shot jump shots on an empty court, wearing a white t-shirt and a broad smile. A few days later, the Baltimore native would commit to come play point guard for the Illini.

The event drew a huge, thunderous crowd, and though the fans in attendance lost some steam during the buildup, as the Illinois women's team was introduced and played a brief scrimmage, the atmosphere was electric when Weber's Illini took the court. The real show came when senior Luther Head outlasted freshman Calvin Brock in the dunk contest, and when the Illini played their first

Just as Illinois prepared in the preseason to leap over its competition, Luther Head jumps over Dee Brown in the slam dunk contest at Illini Basketball Madness. *John Dixon/The News-Gazette*

public scrimmage, wowing the orange-clad with a dazzling three-point barrage.

"It's excellent," Brown said afterward as he signed autographs for dozens of fans. "It just shows you how excited everybody around here is for basketball."

But while fans had gotten their first glimpse of Illinois in a public display of affection, the season had begun in earnest hours before, during a workout closed to all but a handful of reporters and Illinois athletic director Ron Guenther. The day provided an early hint to the split personality that would serve Illinois so well during 2004-05. When the lights were on, the Illini were ready to perform. But underneath the glitz, Illinois was all guts.

"The Madness thing, that's all for show," guard Rich McBride said. "We were all about business."

Fresh Meat

In high school, Calvin Brock was the man. He hadn't drawn the recruiting attention that some of his peers had in the class of 2004, but Brock had proven a late-blooming star at Simeon High School in Chicago, dominating with his high-flying athleticism and silky drives to the basket. But at Illinois, he was just another freshman, which he figured out early on. Over the course of the year, Brock—who chose to redshirt his first season—would be forced by his upperclassman teammates to carry luggage and fetch drinks. But from the time the second practice began, his most tormented times would be on the basketball court.

When they had first set foot on campus, Brown and Williams immediately sent a message that they were unlike other typical freshmen. They would berate senior Brian Cook for taking the ball too softly to the basket. They would bark at sophomore teammate Roger Powell for missing an assignment on defense or failing to set a screen on offense. All the while, they were kept in check by walk-on Jerrance Howard, a guard who rarely played but took it upon himself to break in new teammates with the right mix of tough love and trash talk. His teachings rubbed off on Brown and Williams. In turn, they would pass them on to Brock—with interest.

"I'm going to take the ball from you," Brown would tell Brock. "I'm going to take your rock right now." And then he would.

One Saturday morning in October, when Williams found his path to the basket blocked only by Brock, he took the ball, elevated over the freshman and threw down a vicious one-handed dunk.

"I do this," Williams told a humbled Brock, employing a phrase that would become almost a trademark for the 2005 team. Consider the message delivered.

"They got on me right from the start," Brock said. "It was like they were telling me this is college basketball. This is serious. We're not playing around."

They Do This

The catchphrase was born from a lyric from the rap song, "On My Own," by Lil' Wayne. By midway through the season, no one could remember when it hatched. But after an afternoon practice at the Assembly Hall, as Illinois prepared for a preseason exhibition game, Brown unleashed it, and from there it would escalate.

"I do this!" Brown shouted as he drained jumper after jumper, first from the wing, then moving to the corner. All told, he buried 11 straight, and when the barrage was complete, he left his right hand hanging in the air, wrist still in his shooting follow-through, and repeated his mantra.

"I do this!"

It was simple and direct. It was at once arrogant and understated. In short, it fit the Illini. And it would catch on. I first made it public in an entry on *The News-Gazette's* weblog page. It swept through Illini Nation when fans posted it on the IlliniBoard, the Internet message board devoted to Illinois sports discussions. And by midway through the season, the slogan was on t-shirts, sweatshirts, and even scrolling across the bottom of the video scoreboard at the Assembly Hall.

"Dee just thought it sounded cool," Head said. "Before we knew it, everybody was saying it. It just kind of fit. 'I do this.' It's like, we're all business. We just do it."

The catchphrase caught fire, even though the Illini had no idea just what it was they were about to do: put an exclamation point on the school's 100th year of basketball.

A Bad Break

All Brian Randle wanted was to make an impact on the 2004-05 team. One of Illinois' brightest and hardest-working players, Randle had failed to make a significant splash as a freshman. The six-foot-eight wing player from Peoria Notre Dame high school had shown flashes of his athletic prowess during that freshman year—particularly memorable was a baseline dunk he'd hammered home over a trio of Penn State defenders—but never found a consistent rhythm.

So as his sophomore season dawned, Randle had high hopes. He had developed a reputation over the summer as a tireless worker at the defensive end who could guard a power forward as comfortably as a point guard, and in the opening weeks of practice, Weber repeatedly referred to Randle, whose offseason had been slowed by shoulder surgery, as the team's most improved player. "He's going to surprise some people," Brown said early in the practice season. And he did. But the surprise wasn't the pleasant one Brown had in mind.

One afternoon in November, Randle left practice early after running into a hard screen and tweaking the shoulder he'd had surgically repaired in the offseason. He was taken to the hospital for X-rays, but returned with a clean bill of health the next day. Weber figured his team had dodged a bullet.

Two days later, however, Randle received a bad break to counter the good one. After he missed a shot at the offensive end, Randle was late getting back on defense, giving Roger Powell Jr. a clear path to the basket. Randle hustled back in an effort to block Powell's layup attempt. Too late for the swat, he was whistled for a foul. In frustration, Randle swung wildly at the thick white padding on the wall behind the basket at the Ubben Basketball Complex. He landed a glancing punch with his left hand, and the natural lefty winced in pain immediately.

Teammates—Brown in particular—berated Randle for losing his cool. And they worried. When Randle left the court, he was taken to the hospital for the second time in a week for X-rays. Later in practice, Brown shot free throws while I watched from the upstairs observation deck at Ubben.

"It doesn't look good," Brown said from below. "It's all swollen. It's nasty."

Fortune wouldn't smile twice on Randle. His hand was broken and would require surgery. He would be out at least six weeks, and Weber immediately said Illinois likely would seek a medical redshirt. Randle was doubtful to return. A redshirt season would allow him to retain three full years of eligibility if he did not play again.

The bench reacts as Deron Williams' shot goes in to tie the game near the end of regulation against Arizona. Calvin Brock (center) and Brian Randle (right) became additional cheerleaders for the Illini, as both decided to redshirt during the 2004-05 season. Meanwhile, Warren Carter (left) became a key. *John Dixon/The News-Gazette*

"I felt like an idiot," Randle said. "It's one thing if it's an accident, but that was me losing my temper. I just felt like I let my team down."

Turning a Prophet

Before Illinois had played so much as an exhibition game, the undefeated talk began. The non-conference schedule was diverse—it included teams from the ACC, SEC, Big East, Pac-10, Big 12 and Conference USA—but hardly insurmountable. In private, Weber would tell his team it should set a goal of going unbeaten in pre-conference play. But long before fans knew that, they were talking about perfection.

The Big Ten had been in a downward cycle for several years. Wisconsin and Michigan State both figured to pose threats to Illinois, but even those threats could be conquered. The Spartans had been underachieving since their last Final Four appearance in 2001 and had struggled against the Illini in recent years. Wisconsin, a force since Bo Ryan took over the program, would be without star Devin Harris, who had left school a year early for the NBA draft.

Still, reporters didn't bother to bring up the topic of a perfect season. Not in October. Not so many months from the meat of the schedule. Fans weren't so patient. They asked Weber in the grocery store and at restaurants and in e-mails to his office. They wondered if the team Illinois had put together, with its combination of talent and experience, could make it through an entire year without a blemish. Weber just chuckled at the notion.

"I keep telling our fans we're going to lose a game," Weber said just before the season began. "I haven't decided which one yet."

Something Special

It took outsiders some time to catch on to what was happening in Champaign-Urbana. Weber knew his team had matured since the 2003-04 season; he was aware that he was doing a lot less teaching in practice than he had the year before. And the players themselves could sense something special. But the program was locked down through most of October, allowing only a few media and visitors to see what was happening behind the closed doors at the Ubben Basketball Complex.

One person who got a brief look was Purdue coach Gene Keady. Keady had long been a mentor to Weber, who'd spent 19 years as an assistant under Keady, first at Western Kentucky and then for 18 seasons at Purdue. The two were as close as father and son, and as Keady embarked on his final season with the Boilermakers, he took time out of a packed practice schedule to visit Weber's annual clinic for high school coaches in Illinois. It didn't take a long look at the Illini before Keady could see Weber was onto something.

"It looks like a very good team," Keady would say. "I've been around the Big Ten a long time, and I can't remember ever seeing a three-guard lineup like theirs."

During his visit, though, Keady stole the show. His speech to the assembled high school coaches at Ubben was a riotous, R-rated affair. Though he broke down the Xs and Os of his team's daily practice routine, he also took the opportunity to discuss the changes in the game—and the young men who play it—over his 30-plus years in coaching. There was a time during his junior college days, Keady revealed, when he took only basketball players who participated in other sports—football or track, for example—on his team. He also used to force all of his players to join the Fellowship of Christian Athletes, a policy that wouldn't fly today.

Mostly, though, Keady talked about the relationship with players and their parents, a relationship that he called the biggest change in coaching over the course of his career. "These days, all the kids are on Prozac," Keady said. "We had Prozac when I was a kid. We called it a [bleepin'] stick." The room erupted in laughter. Even Weber, who'd long since heard Keady's best one-liners, cracked a wide smile.

Six months later, Weber's true feelings for his mentor would come out in a warm, emotional ceremony during Keady's final visit to the Assembly Hall as Purdue's coach. But on that October Friday night, his affection for the coaching legend—as it so often did during his first two years at Illinois—made him a target for verbal jabs from his quick-witted players.

As Keady gave his rousing speech to the high school coaches at Ubben, Weber's players strolled in from the locker room, their practice complete, and a free Friday night awaiting them. Weber watched intently as Keady worked the room, and as he did, Dee Brown wandered over and put his arm around his coach.

"Awww," Brown whispered, nodding toward Keady. "Look at your daddy."

All Grown Up

As preseason practice progressed, it was clear to Weber that he was coaching a different team than he had in 2003-04, when players still harbored loyalties to Bill Self and were resistant to Weber's teachings. From the first few days of practice, it was obvious how much the Illini had grown up. Weber's "Perfection" drill was an elaborate up-and-down the court drill that focused on lay-ups, shooting, and passing. It often took the Illini 11 or 12 minutes to complete the drill in the fall of 2003; this year, however, the team routinely wrapped it up within the seven-minute deadline that Weber put on his best, most experienced teams at Southern Illinois.

Though the handful of new players on the roster—Brock, Shaun Pruitt, and Illinois State transfer Marcus Arnold—took time to learn the nuances of Weber's motion offense, the veterans appeared to have mastered it in the offseason.

"It's totally different the second time around," James Augustine said. "He knows what to expect from us, we know what to expect from him. It's a lot better situation. I think everybody came out for practice focused, ready to play, and ready to prove that we are a great team."

That didn't mean that things always went smoothly. During one early practice Weber, incensed over his team's lack of defensive effort, stopped play, and began shouting, "You guys are going to screw around on defense like this, and Gonzaga's going to kick your ass! Or Wake Forest is going to kick your ass! Remember last year! Remember Providence!"

The Providence game was the first in a series of low points during Weber's first season in Champaign. Unprepared for the Friars' intensity—and their confounding zone defense—Illinois looked sluggish all night and suffered an embarrassing 70-51 loss at Madison Square Garden.

"Don't make it take you getting your ass kicked to learn a lesson!" he shouted. "Learn your lessons now! That's what practice is for!"

In trying to drive home his point, Weber stripped the ball from Deron Williams, standing at the top of the key to soak in his coach's tirade. Weber threw the ball from the three-point line to the wall behind the opposite basket at Ubben. When a manager retrieved the ball and gave it to Williams, Weber yanked it out of his point guard's hands a second time and threw it again, the ball making a loud thump as it bounced off the back wall.

"Sometimes he gets like that," Williams said. "He just has to make sure we're listening."

2

THE THREE AMIGOS

When he'd recruited Luther Head, and then Dee Brown and Deron Williams, Bill Self knew he was on to something. Head, a quiet but athletic slasher from Manley High School in Chicago whose jump shot hadn't caught up with the rest of his game, wasn't the most highly regarded recruit. A year later, Brown and Williams were superstar recruits at the point guard position whom few coaches expected to land at the same school. Self had a vision for the three guards. But even he didn't see what lay ahead for them.

"I knew they were really, really good players," Self said. "But did I have any idea they were going to be what they were? I can't say that. I think you could look at it with Dee and Deron and see what they could give you down the road. What really made it work is how much Luther improved over the course of his four years."

Indeed, by the time Head reached his senior year, healthy and happy—and there were times when either seemed a remote possibility—it was clear that he had grown into something no one could have expected. He was an elite player. He was perhaps the Big Ten's most dangerous three-point shooter. And, in truth, he was what no one ever expected: a point guard.

"We're all three point guards," Williams said. "That's what makes [us] so tough to defend. We all do different things, but you can give any of us the ball and we can handle it. You look at

Michigan State, they don't have one true point guard. We've got three."

If ever in college hoops history a team had employed a three-point guard offense—and done it with such staggering success—no one seemed to remember. ESPN analyst Steve Lavin often likened Brown, Williams, and Head to the Arizona backcourt of Miles Simon, Mike Bibby, and Jason Terry that helped the Wildcats win the 1997 NCAA title. But even that comparison didn't hold up; Terry played a backup point guard role. Brown, Williams, and Head shared center stage.

"It's amazing, because you can't find one decent point guard in college basketball," said Chris Ekstrand, a consultant with the NBA. "And then you'd watch Illinois, and they had three of them. I'd never seen anything like it."

Dee Brown (left), Deron Williams (center), and Luther Head were a trio of stars for the Illini. Their performance on the court was bolstered by their friendship off of it. The most productive guard trio in the history of the program combined to average 41.8 points, 15.1 assists, 4.5 steals, and 7.3 three-pointers per game. *Darrell Hoemann/The News-Gazette*

It may take some time before anyone else sees anything like it again, because Brown, Head, and Williams weren't just outstanding guards. They were a true trio, a group of players whose on- and off-court chemistry was such that none clamored for credit and none put himself ahead of the other two—or the team. When Head, quiet and reserved, got off to a superstar's start, Brown and Williams were the first to hype him as an All-America candidate. When Brown opened his closet, a Williams jersey hung among the legendary NBA and NFL stars. "He's the best point guard in America," Brown would say of Williams. Whether or not it was true hardly mattered.

"When [Brown] said that, you knew [the Illini] had something going," said ESPN analyst Fran Fraschilla. "He could've said, 'We're the best combo,' or 'He's right there with me,' but when he gave his teammate that much credit, I could've told you right then that they were going to have a great, great year."

Deron Williams:
The Watchful Eye

Like a lot of kids who grow up without a father, Williams had an unbreakable bond with his mother. Unlike a lot of kids, Williams had a mother who could more than hold her own on the basketball court.

"She taught me everything," Williams said. "She taught me how to shoot, how to pass. She taught me about defense."

Denise Smith had been a standout collegiate player at Liberty College in West Virginia, where she met Williams' father, also a basketball player there. His father isn't a subject Williams discusses now. As far as he's concerned, Denise is the sole source of his basketball lineage.

When he was a kid, Williams was exposed to all kinds of sports. Smith wanted him occupied in every season, and though he immediately showed a knack for basketball, he also was a standout wrestler.

"He was a natural athlete," Smith said. "We could tell right away."

But there was something else. From an early age, Williams began to exhibit the qualities that eventually would make him a standout point guard. He was a natural leader. He was quietly confident with a basketball in his hands. And he was wildly observant. Weber learned shortly after coming to Illinois that he wouldn't have to worry about remembering what he had told his team. No matter what Weber said, Williams would remember it for him. By the time he reached college, Williams had grown physically, but his mental capacity also had expanded. He'd become something of an on-court court reporter.

"You could say something one day and six months later say something in practice that contradicted that, and he'd say, 'But Coach, six months ago, you said it was the other way,'" Weber said. "It's uncanny. He notices everything, and he forgets nothing."

When I showed up at practice once with a new digital recorder, Williams noticed. The same thing occurred on the day that I came to practice wearing glasses instead of my contacts. Get new shoes? Williams will spot them. Change your haircut? It won't get by him.

"I think it's that point guard thing," Williams said. "I've always got my eyes open."

That attention to detail impressed NBA scouts, many of whom rated Williams as the first or second best point guard in college basketball.

Dee Brown: The Poster Child

If you wanted to see Brown's influence—on local kids or on college basketball—you needed only watch him a short while. You could come to a game at the Assembly Hall and see the headbands and the high socks. You could watch a high school game in Central Illinois and see the orange mouthpieces. You could watch any game on ESPN and see that ubiquitous jersey tug, otherwise known as "popping the jersey."

That signature move became Brown's lasting contribution to the basketball scene in 2004-05. Whether or not he was the first to institute it seems almost a moot point. He brought it to the masses, and it caught on. Brown's simple move—looping his thumbs underneath the jersey to raise the "ILLINOIS" across the front into the air—spread like wildfire through the Big Ten, the NCAA, and even into women's basketball and the NBA. Brown debuted the move at Purdue, burying a second-half three-pointer then sprinting back down the court with the jersey raised toward the Illinois fans in the upper deck at Mackey Arena.

"That's who I play for," Brown said. "I'm trying to get our program, our school more on the map, get more recognition."

Brown always did his part on that front. Like Self, Weber called Brown the "poster child" of Illinois basketball, and his impact on the program stretched well beyond the court. The *Sports Illustrated* cover kid gave Illinois a face that fans—and more importantly, recruits—could identify with.

"He's like the governor down in Illinois," said Chester Frazier, the high school point guard who met Brown on a recruiting visit and later signed with the Illini. "I just knew right away he'd be a fun guy to play with. I wanted to be on his team."

Luther Head: The Quiet One

Though Head and Brown grew to be close friends during their time in Champaign, the two couldn't be more different. Where Brown was outgoing, Head was introverted. Where Brown was a social butterfly, Head often—particularly during his senior year—spent weekends alone in his room.

"I'd just have a Blockbuster weekend," said Head, whose most viewed movies included *Ocean's 11* and *Scarface*. "I've always been that way. When I was growing up, my mom would be like, 'Why don't you ever go outside?'"

Even as a kid, Head kept quiet. But he had his dreams. At an early age, when he discovered his knack for basketball, he began to look at the game as a way to get his family out of poverty. His mother, Bonnie, raised five children mostly on her own. When Head was in high school, she met and eventually married his high school coach, Bo Delaney, who worked long hours at a Chicago factory, mostly at night. Delaney made things better for the family. They moved into a larger apartment, and, Head said, "finally had a little bit of money." More importantly, he played the role of surrogate father to Head.

"He was my dad way before he and my mom got married," Head said. "He made everything better. My mother was happy again. I started to see smiles on her face sometimes. It just made everything better."

Still, with four younger siblings, Head knew his mother would work hard all her life to support her family—unless he could do more than his share. So when Head was on the playground or alone in the apartment, he would dream of one day playing in the NBA. When he was a sophomore at Manley High School, he and his best friend, Will Bynum, a star at Crane Tech, got identical NBA logo tattoos on their forearms.

"We both dreamed of making it," said Bynum, who went on to play at Arizona and then Georgia Tech. "And when times got rough, we could look down at those tattoos and remember what we played for. That was our inspiration."

Head looked to realize his dream come June, when the NBA draft would be held.

The Trio's Roots

While Williams was growing up hundreds of miles away, Brown and Head were spending their formative years just miles apart in Chicago, separated by a stretch of city blocks you could span in a short bus ride. But for kids, anything outside walking distance might as well be a state away. And so, while Brown and Head knew each other's names and faces, for them to actually meet would take time. That meant Brown and Head's friendship was casual.

"I think I was about nine the first time I saw him play," Brown said. "I was like, 'This kid is for real.' But we didn't really get to be real, real close friends until I came to Illinois, when he was a sophomore. Me, him and Deron, we'd stay in the same place, we'd hang out all the time."

Brown and Williams had forged a bond over the phone during the recruiting process. Brown had committed to the Illini first, then set about helping Self and his staff convince Williams that the two could share the court. Williams had shown no desire to play alongside another point guard, and no other school had asked him to. When Jarrett Jack committed to Georgia Tech the week before Williams' scheduled visit to Atlanta, the Yellow Jackets called Williams and pulled his scholarship offer. Kansas had been interested, but only if it hadn't landed Aaron Miles (which it did)—same for North Carolina and Raymond Felton.

"It was like a process of elimination that I ended up at Illinois," Williams said. "Or I guess you could say it was fate."

Still, there was scarcely any sign of what was in store for Illinois' trio. Brown, Williams, and Head hardly seemed fated for Illinois basketball greatness. At least not as a threesome. Almost immediately, Brown and Williams made an impact: Williams with his size, strength, and feel for the game—"He knew more than a guy his age should know," Head said—and Brown with his blinding quickness. Two weeks into practice their freshman year at Illinois, Williams proclaimed of Brown, "I hate guarding his little ass."

But Head, plagued then as he had so often been his freshman year by a sports hernia, wasn't putting his same imprint on the game. He had his moments, but he played with intense pain that took away his leaping ability—until that point, the strength of his game—and made simply running up and down the court a taxing process.

"I thought I was never gonna be healthy again," Head said.

Offseason surgery would put his body right heading into his junior year. But that's when everything went wrong.

Obstacle Course

The season Brown, Williams, and Head posted in Bruce Weber's second season at Illinois almost happened in his first. At least it seemed like it might. All three players entered 2003-04 healthy, and while Brown and Williams had made the strides you'd expect between a freshman and sophomore season, Head, too, had taken his game to another level. It showed right from the start of practice.

"There are days," Weber said then, "when he's the best player on the floor."

Until he was taken off it. Late in the preseason, Weber announced that Head would miss the first four games of the season—two exhibitions and two regular-season games—for an unspecified violation of team rules. Teammates Rich McBride and Aaron Spears also were suspended. Weber refused to elaborate, but it was clear that the cause for the suspension was wearing on the Illinois coach. And when the alleged reason for the suspension came down, it was the talk of Champaign-Urbana.

The father of an Illinois student told *The News-Gazette* that Head, McBride and Spears had been involved in a break-in at his son's Champaign apartment, and that the Illinois players and other men had stolen thousands of dollars' worth of electronics, DVDs, and clothing. Charges never were filed against the three players—a controversial decision made by the Champaign County State's Attorney in part at the request of the victims—but Head was on thin ice with his new coach.

He couldn't stay off of it. Later in the season, Head was suspended again, this time after being arrested for driving on a suspended license. Weber sat him for two more games and said that Head had two strikes. He wouldn't get another. In a private meeting during that suspension, Head went to Weber not to appeal for a speedy return, but to make Weber an offer.

"I told him if I was being a distraction, I'd leave," Head said. And he meant it.

"None of us even knew [about the meeting]," Brown said. "That's the crazy thing about it. I think we would've tried to talk him out of it. He just never told us."

Head only told Weber. And to his surprise, Weber wouldn't accept his resignation.

"I don't want you to leave," the coach told his player. "I want you to change."

Head vowed then that he would. By all accounts, he did. During his senior year, Head didn't distract anyone—save perhaps the NBA scouts who'd come to see Brown and Williams. By the midway point of 2004-05, Head was an All-America candidate and one of the most talked-about players in the nation for no reason other than his play.

"If you think about it, he's what college basketball is all about," Weber said. "He grew up. To go through all he's gone through and come out a better player, a college graduate, a better person? That's what you hope for."

Who's Mr. Clutch?

Long before the NCAA tournament, before Williams made the biggest shot of the season—perhaps any season—for Illinois against Arizona, I asked Brown, Williams, and Head about just such a situation. Crucial game. Crucial possession. Who gets the ball?

"Whoever's open," Williams said.

"Yup," Head agreed. "Whoever gets it."

"I'd say either one of those two dudes," Brown said. "I'm not really a big-time shooter like that."

"You're shooting, like, 50 percent from three," Williams said, punching Brown in the arm.

"But I'm sayin', though, I ain't no big-time shooter like that," Brown said. "I ain't never made a shot like that."

In fact, Brown hadn't buried a game-winner in college. His last one had come in a high school game at Proviso East, a play that's featured on Brown's high school highlight video, a feature presentation I once saw in Brown's mother's apartment the summer before his senior year. In it, Brown dazzled not only as an undersized point guard, but also as a fleet-footed quarterback on the Proviso East football team.

"Everybody's seen the video," Weber said. "I don't think he plays it for people, but I've heard that guys just want to see it."

Despite documented proof of a game-winning buzzer-beater, though, Brown insisted that faced with that situation, he'd sooner give the ball to Head or Williams.

"Put the ball in Deron's hands, put him and Luther on the same side of the floor," Brown said. "Deron's gonna create something."

"Yeah," Williams smiled. "I'll get it to one of them."

The Pied Pipers

There is a look that Weber gives when he's disappointed in practice, a glare that he shoots a player's way when words won't capture the mood. He also has that voice, that perpetually hoarse, nails-on-a-chalkboard screech that by midway through the season sounds as if it's been working non-stop for months (which it has). Several members of the Illinois roster had tried their hand at impersonating Weber's voice, but never in front of the coach.

"Oh, they do it," Weber said.

Brown and Williams, not surprisingly, are the ringleaders. "It's pretty funny," Brown said. "But I can't [do it for] you. Maybe one day." When the eligibility is used up, perhaps.

Illinois' guard trio were go-to guys for more than just clutch shots: they were the guys with the gags and the nicknames. Brown alone created several, including Rich McBride's dual monikers, "Foots" (from the foot problems that caused his unorthodox walk) and "The Veteran." ("He looks like he's 40," Williams explained.) More than Illinois' best players, Brown, Williams, and Head became the program's leaders in every sense of the word.

"Those are the guys," James Augustine said. "They're the leaders of this team, the guys we always look to. I mean, they score points, but they set everybody up, they make everybody better. On the court, in the locker room, vocally, whatever—they're the leaders."

Having three players who could lead the way—and do it in such divergent styles—was a contrast from what Weber had seen upon taking the Illinois job, when he worried that there wasn't anyone to fill the role of coach on the court. Brown and Williams had been among the Big Ten's best assist men as freshmen, unselfish guards who could score or set up teammates. But that had been under a different coach, and Weber wondered if the duo would buy into his system and lead the way as sophomores. Brown was especially resistant to Weber's system at first, creating rumblings about a rift. But once he bought in—and once Head's legal problems were put in the past—Illinois' trio was on the same page.

"We never doubted their abilities," Weber said. "I remember the first day we had them in the spring when I first took the job, we watched them, and we thought, 'Wow.' Chris Lowery and I were talking; we had run the motion offense at Southern Illinois, and we had guys who could come off screens and do some things, but [with] these guys, it was a different level. Deron could bully you, Luther could jump over you, and Dee could blow right by you."

Admiration Society

As that versatility helped Illinois pile up wins, it won the Illini some fans across the country. Many of them were coaching Illinois' opponents. Gene Keady called the trio the best guard threesome he'd seen in the Big Ten. Minnesota's Dan Monson said that shutting down Brown, Head, and Williams on the same night was "virtually impossible." And no less an authority than UCLA legend John Wooden praised Illinois for the unselfish team play that began in the backcourt.

"Their three guards are going to be consistent," Indiana coach Mike Davis said. "I don't care what defense you run or what you try to do."

"I love those three guys," Michigan State coach Tom Izzo said. "I mean, when I have to play against 'em, I can't stand 'em. But to me, those are three All-Big Ten guys and three guys who really make that team go with their unselfishness and their leadership. I don't see how you could not love 'em."

Or at least admire them. Coaches all year were confounded by trying to guard the trio. If Brown's speed didn't burn you, wily Williams would make the perfect pass. And Head sank so many backbreaking three-pointers, opposing coaches learned that backing off Illinois' "other" guard was no option. The three helped the Illini set a school record for three-pointers in a season (344 made), but that was just one aspect of the backcourt's three-dimensional game.

"We knew they could shoot the ball from three," Gonzaga coach Mark Few said after Illinois buried his Zags 89-72 in November. "But they're so good at moving that you're chasing them around. So you either get beat by the twos or you get beat by the threes."

That all three of Illinois' starting guards had such a variety of weapons made defending the Illini a nightmare—and made watching the Illini a thrill for fans and analysts alike.

"In a day and age when we always seem to be talking about specialization among players, it's unique to see three guys who do so many things well," Fraschilla said. "They can all play the point. They can all score. They all seem to have checked their egos at the door."

Competitive Compatriots

As Head, Brown, and Williams grew as players and people, they grew closer as friends, too. In an age when Shaquille O'Neal and Kobe Bryant had famously feuded en route to championship success in the NBA, the Illini were well-versed in the adage that you didn't have to get along off the court to succeed on it. But they didn't buy it.

"I think what makes us work is that we're unselfish," Head said. "If we didn't like each other so much, I don't know if it would be that way."

It helped that Head had spent his first three years in college as a supporting player, first to Frank Williams and Cory Bradford, then to Brian Cook. And that Brown and Williams had played their high school days alongside teammates who were as highly regarded as they were—if not more so. For Williams, the headline-stealer was Bracey Wright, his more hotly recruited teammate at The Colony High School in Texas. Williams, he admitted, was considered "Bracey's sidekick" when the two played prep hoops together. As a senior, Brown was the star attraction of his Proviso East High School team in Maywood, Illinois. But teammate Shannon Brown—a year younger than Dee—was considered by many to be the better prospect.

"I always played on a team with killers," Brown said. "And not even a big man, but another guard. I always wanted to play on a team like that."

Coach Bruce Weber (far left) knew from day one that he had something special in his dazzling backcourt: Dee Brown (left), Luther Head (center), and Deron Williams (right). Here, Illini's leaders celebrate receiving the top overall spot in the 2005 NCAA tournament. *AP/WWP*

With their press-sharing pedigree, Brown, Williams, and Head had been groomed for the kind of season they shared in 2004-05. But beyond their willingness to share the spotlight, Illinois' backcourt trio worked because of the friendship they'd forged in three seasons together.

"Teams who get along off the court have better chemistry," Weber said. "They don't have to be with each other every minute, but you want them to get along. Our team seems to really enjoy each other, and those three have a tendency to stick together more than any of them."

It was a bond formed not only of shared experience—Brown and Williams, for example, both had fathered children at a young age—but of deep-seeded similarity. Mostly, they said, it sprang from competition. From ping pong to poker, PlayStation to practice—

and especially practice—Brown, Head, and Williams competed at everything.

"Pie-eatin' contest, whatever," Head said.

It gave them a thrill, brought them closer together. And Weber hardly dissuaded the competitive nature. Quite the contrary, he fostered it, often splitting up his three guards in practice for competitive drills. Winner gets water, loser sprints.

"They're so competitive, it seems like at least one of them is mad at us every day in practice," Weber said.

But the competition carried over well outside routine practices. Brown and Williams had a heated series of ping pong games. Brown would boast that he was the team's video game ace, and he'd get no argument. But Head could clean out his teammates at poker. And Williams? He won the arguments, which were plenty.

"Every day," Williams said. "We argue every day."

As in most every situation, Head would stay quiet when the arguments flared up. But Brown and Williams would go after it on any range of topics. Best rapper. Best NBA player. Best road-trip dinner spot. It never stopped.

"I usually win," Williams said.

"He does," Brown said. "Whenever we argue, he gets on the Internet and breaks out all the facts. He's always got numbers or something like that. I just go with my heart and argue. He's the one who does, like, research and all that."

Their competitive nature sometimes—though rarely—led to words being exchanged on the court. Typically, though, bygones were bygones the moment Weber blew his whistle.

"Nobody takes it personally," Williams said. "We're all friends."

Opposites Attract

Despite their deep friendship and obvious similarities, Illinois' trio of guards freely admitted their considerable differences. Brown is a chatterbox, who—barring his occasional foul mood—loves to chat up fans and reporters. He's the headband-wearing, jersey-popping face of the Illinois program.

"It don't matter if you've got a tape recorder or a microphone or whatever," Brown said. "I just like to talk. I want to meet everybody."

Williams is more stoic and less jittery, but still effusive. Insightful and articulate, he was second only to Brown among the media's favorite interview targets. Head's the quiet one, the "silent assassin," as Williams called him. Their differences had led them all to the same place by 2004-05, and the future might well hold a similar path. Brown hopes to join Williams and Head in the NBA following his senior season. And though Brown often said he wasn't certain he'd be able to do just that, Williams and Head dismissed his naysaying as "reverse psychology."

What of the long-term future, though? Asked that question one day during the season—as they nibbled on post-practice chicken wings on the court at Ubben—the trio gave it their customary consideration, thinking carefully before producing answers. Brown had always seemed tailor-made for television, but he insisted that he'd someday be a coach, perhaps at the college level.

"I've seen so many dudes play, I think I could help people out," Brown said. "Make them better players."

Williams laughed.

"I can't see no coach with no braids," Williams said. "You're going to have to cut your hair."

"I'm going to cut my hair anyway," Brown said.

"There he goes again," Head laughed.

Too quiet to be a media analyst, Head said he, too, would fancy coaching. If only he thought he could handle it.

"I don't think it's my personality," he said.

"Nope," Brown said.

Williams, too, saw himself as a coach somewhere down the road. Maybe.

"I'm going to be a coach," Williams said. "But then again, I'll tell you something: If I have a great career in the NBA—like, 10, 12 years—I'm going to lay down somewhere for the rest of my life. In the bed. I might not get up. Except to eat."

Wherever he ends up, Williams predicted, Brown and Head would be close by. The three figure they'll stand up in each other's weddings someday. And before the 2004-05 season ended, they'd already made plans to take trips together once all three wrapped up their collegiate experience.

"We're gonna go back to Vegas when it's not a basketball trip and we can go out and do stuff," Head said. "We're definitely making plans."

They have plenty of time.

"These are my guys. We're going to be friends a long time," Williams said. "I'm going to know these guys when I'm old and gray."

3

ROUNDING OUT THE ROSTER

*I*f it's true that a team takes on the personality of its coach, then the 2004-05 Fighting Illini were bound to be a schizophrenic bunch. Three coaches, after all, had played a part in constructing the team, and the players on the roster were as disparate as they were talented.

There were two senior starters in Illinois' lineup. One, Roger Powell Jr., became a licensed minister before the start of his senior season. The other, Luther Head, still had a probation officer stemming from a string of traffic violations racked up during his sophomore and junior years.

"We're different, but it works," Dee Brown said. "We're a real close-knit team. We pray together, we go out together. Even in the offseason, we all go out to the movies, go bowling. We're tight, even though we have a lot of different personalities."

Those wildly different personalities were reflections of the three men who brought them into the program. It began with Lon Kruger, who signed Nick Smith and secured a verbal commitment from Powell. It continued with Bill Self, who put together the bulk of the roster, including juniors Brown, Deron Williams, and James Augustine, who would help form the core of the team. And it continued with Weber, who gets the credit for the on-court results in 2004-05 but recruited only one player who saw action, freshman forward Shaun Pruitt.

The knock that Weber was "winning with other people's players" never bothered the coach. He had, after all, molded players who were recruited by two previous coaches—and coached for a year or more by Self—into a cohesive unit that would go on to dominate college basketball for most of the season. That was no small feat, given just how unique a mix of personalities Weber had inherited.

The Rev

The signs came in the spring of 2004, sometimes on television, sometimes at church. Roger Powell Jr. would have a question, and then he'd have his answer. He'd wonder about the direction his life was taking, and a pastor's sermon would give him a new path. He'd struggle with a problem in his everyday life, and the answer to his problem would come during a show on the Trinity Broadcast Network.

It would be simple to say that Powell watched the Mel Gibson film *The Passion of the Christ* and his life was changed. And it would be true. But for Powell, it wasn't that simple. Nor that easy to understand.

Strangers would approach him on the street, not to ask for an autograph but to tell him, "God has something for you." And though Powell admits he was "freaked out" when it happened, it didn't take him long to reach a conclusion that eased his mind.

"It was my calling," Powell said.

And so Powell followed it. Just a few weeks before practice started in his senior basketball season, he became a licensed minister (becoming ordained is a process that will take years). Months before that, he'd given his life—and most of his CDs, too—to God. He purged the CD shelf: Out with most of the rap, in with gospel, a music he'd always listened to but suddenly found himself hearing in a whole new way.

"The day after I saw *The Passion of the Christ*," Powell said, "I was just like, 'Jesus did all of this for me, and I'm listening to *this* stuff?'"

But taking coarse language out of his speakers wasn't enough. Powell removed it from his vocabulary, too. One afternoon during

Roger Powell Jr., "The Rev," points to the heavens after cutting the net following Illinois' win over Arizona in the Elite Eight.
Darrell Hoemann/The News-Gazette

an early season practice, he took a hard foul and his backside hit the floor with a thunderous thump. Powell rolled on the court in pain.

"Shoot," he moaned. And again, "Shoot!"

"I kind of wanted to say something [worse], but it's been so long since I cursed, it didn't even come to me," he would say the next day.

When he got his minister's license, Powell had only recently turned 21. He turned his back on alcohol just as he was legally able to buy it.

"He gave himself over to God," Brown said. "That's not easy to do."

Powell's theory—but not his motivation—was that his conversion would pay dividends on the court as well. Though his game didn't change dramatically in his senior year, Powell said he played with an inner peace that was entirely new. Basketball wasn't any less important to him. But his faith had become so significant it dwarfed everything else.

"It felt like I could just play," Powell said. "I had a new sense of why I was playing basketball. It was to serve the Lord."

And every chance he got, Powell would display his newfound passion.

He would sink a three-point shot—an offensive weapon he'd all but abandoned during his junior year, but which returned for his senior season—and he'd look to the heavens. Illinois would warm up for a game, and Powell would pray. And when the Illini beat Arizona to advance to the Final Four—a win that seemed to have no explanation short of divine intervention—Powell climbed a ladder to snip his piece of the celebratory net and raised a finger toward the sky in praise.

"Roger was our spiritual leader," Head said. "It was great."

The Approachable One

In a community as small and basketball-crazed as Champaign-Urbana, it's virtually impossible for a player to have a big night and not get pats on the back the next day. At the sandwich shop buying lunch. At Wal-Mart picking up groceries. It's hard to avoid the praise.

James Augustine received a different kind of support. Maybe Augustine was just more approachable than the rest. Maybe his affable nature and everyman attitude made him easy to be honest with. Whatever the case, Augustine knew exactly what to expect after each big scoring or rebounding night.

"People would come up to me right out in public and say, 'Why don't you play like that all the time?'" Augustine said. "I hear that constantly."

You might think that Augustine's inconsistency is a sore spot, that he'd tire of hearing fans telling him that he should be more assertive night in and night out. You'd be wrong. In fact, those sorts of kick-in-the-pants encouragements only made Augustine feel that much more at home.

Dale Augustine, James' father, is a high school football coach in Mokena, Illinois. He's also his son's toughest basketball critic. When junior James opened the Big Ten season with 21 points and 10 rebounds against Ohio State—his first 20-point game of the season—Dale saw me on the way to the media room and said, "About time."

Following the Illinois players' press conference, I passed that nugget on to James, who wasn't surprised. "He's always been that way," Augustine said of his dad. "It motivates me."

The father dished it out, and the son came to enjoy taking it. A simple, "Good game" was nice, but a critique—an analysis not of James' statistics but of his effort—was Dale's specialty.

And if that wasn't enough, there were strangers at Wal-Mart to push the right buttons. On campus, though, there weren't many strangers to James Augustine. One of the most popular Illini among the student body, he was hard to spot alone. Walking on the Quad or heading out to dinner, you were likely to see Augustine with company in tow.

"Everybody knows him," said Matt McCumber, the Illinois student manager who became one of Augustine's closest friends. "Everybody likes him. He's always joking around. People just laugh at him all the time. Everybody comes up to him and talks to him."

In fact, folks got so comfortable with Augustine that they had no problem talking to him about even the most delicate matters.

James Augustine is hugged by adoring fans after the team arrived back in Champaign following its victory against Arizona in the Elite Eight.
Heather Coit/The News-Gazette

Take, for example, the perplexing question of his ethnicity. For years now, Augustine has been asked at least once a week about his racial makeup. Talk to anyone who knows him, and they've been asked the question. And they—like the man in question—laugh every time, because Augustine's ethnicity isn't nearly as convoluted as some people seem to think it is.

"I'm just a white guy," Augustine said. "I have two white parents. People don't believe it, but it's true."

When Augustine says "people don't believe it," he's not kidding. As a freshman, he was asked to run for African-American homecoming king at Illinois. He politely declined, on account of being a self-professed "white dude."

"People were like, 'Are you sure one of your grandpas isn't black or something?'" Augustine said. "And I was like, 'I'm pretty sure.'"

He laughs telling the story. He laughs a lot, but nothing gets him rolling quite like this topic, one he's rarely asked about by reporters but is completely comfortable discussing.

"People would call me up and ask if I was half-something or other, and when I say 'I'm white,' you hear people in the background cheering like, 'Yeah! You owe me $20! I told you he was white!'" Augustine said. "My parents laugh at it. On the IlliniBoard (a fan internet message board), some people think I'm Mexican. I've heard Dominican, Arabian. Coach (Wayne) McClain calls me 'Cosmopolitan.' He makes fun of me all the time."

The Professor

If you asked Jack Ingram which of his Illinois classes gave him the hardest time, he wouldn't hesitate in answering. "Solid State Electronic Devices," he would say. And you would wonder if this guy really was a basketball player. Perhaps no player in recent Illinois history shattered stereotypes like Ingram, a true student-athlete who took his studies as seriously as his bone-crunching picks. And those *were* serious business.

Though he became a go-to guy for clutch jump shots, and though he was among the most cerebral players on Illinois' roster— Weber said no player other than Deron Williams grasped his motion offense faster—Ingram transferred from Tulsa with a well-earned reputation for toughness. Nowhere on his resume did it mention his smarts.

One day in practice during Self's last season, Ingram (redshirting after his transfer, per NCAA rules) dislocated a finger so severely that the bone poked through the skin on his hand. Brian Cook took one look at the injury and nearly fainted. Several players looked as though they might lose their lunch on the practice court.

Jack Ingram, known to teammates as "The Professor," became an essential part of Illinois' bench during the 2004-05 season. From his key shots at Wisconsin to his valuable play in the championship game, Ingram provided much-needed depth for the Illini frontcourt.
John Dixon/The News-Gazette

Not Jack. He calmly pushed the bone back under the skin and walked to the trainer's room, as though he had an appointment.

"That," Self said then, "is what I call tough."

But Ingram was mentally tough, too. He would have to be to put up with all the drama he endured in college. Recruited by Self at Tulsa, Ingram ended up playing there first for Buzz Peterson and then for John Phillips. After two seasons at Tulsa, Ingram transferred to Illinois to play for Self. After Ingram's redshirt year, Self left for Kansas, and Weber was hired to replace him. That meant Ingram would have four different head coaches in five years of college basketball.

"His junior year, his mom called me a couple of times," Weber said. "She said, 'Please make sure you stay for Jack's senior year. I think he's starting to get a complex.'"

A few coaching changes, though, are child's play compared to all that Ingram balanced in his three-year stay in Champaign. Besides learning two completely different offenses, he was busy learning to be an electrical engineer. He'd put in long hours on the practice court, then retreat to his apartment, crack the books, and start working away at Solid State Electronic Devices.

"It has a bunch of modern-type physics, quantum physics mixed in with a lot of statistics stuff, and you're talking about semi-conductors and MOS devices," Ingram said, as cooly as he might discuss Wisconsin's swing offense. "The theory itself is hard to get, and if you ever get past the theory, the math that backs up the theory is even harder. So it hits you with the one-two punch."

Ingram packed a little one-two punch of his own: an enforcer on the court and an engineer off it.

"We started calling him 'The Professor,'" Brown said, "because he knows everything."

The Enigma

Long after the technical fouls prompted by his short fuse have been forgotten, and his no-holds-barred diatribes are distant memories, Nick Smith will be remembered. He'll have left a lasting legacy at Illinois. That is, unless a seven-foot-three guy comes along.

"Oh, God—'The tallest player in Illinois basketball history,'" the seven-foot-two Smith said. "How long until I live that down? How could we ever forget that one?"

True enough, Smith was the tallest Illini ever to don the orange and blue—and the title followed him everywhere. If an out-of-towner wrote a story on Smith, you'd find it in the copy somewhere. If he stepped to the free throw line in a game or knocked down an open 15-footer, it was a safe bet you'd hear the color commentator throwing the title around. It was right there, every year, in his Illinois media guide bio.

Smith's height, though, is a short story. There's a much longer one behind his five-year stay at Illinois. Signed by Kruger and coached first by Self, Smith had all the makings of a matchup nightmare. Never a dominant post presence—even by his senior year, he weighed only about 240 pounds—Smith could stretch defenses and pull big defenders away from the basket with his outside shooting. During a game at Purdue in his junior year, he sank two three-pointers in overtime to help Illinois win a Big Ten title-clinching game. As a senior, he helped seal a win at Iowa with a three from the corner as the shot clock winded down in the game's closing minutes.

But for every highlight, Smith seemed to have a low or two, particularly in the Weber era. The two had a problematic relationship that sometimes played out in the media. Smith once said that while Self was a player's friend, Weber was comparable to "my high school math teacher." And Weber, tired of what he called a negative attitude, once said of Smith, "He's just being Nick. He needs to learn not to be."

Smith admitted he could be difficult at times. And though his minutes were drastically reduced his senior year, he rarely complained. On occasion, Smith would question his playing time in public discussions with the media, but such boat-rocking was rare. And that, Smith said, was by design.

"When you've got a good thing going," he said, "you don't want to be the one who rocks the boat."

He sometimes did, though. In his junior year, he infuriated teammates with an untimely technical foul in a blowout loss at Wisconsin. And his temper got the better of him his senior year

Nick Smith's stay in Champaign will be remembered for more than just being "the tallest player in Illinois history." The seven-foot-two center frustrated fans with his inconsistency and his attitude, but he also hit some big shots during his career. *John Dixon/The News-Gazette*

when he tossed a ball to the opposite end of the court after he was whistled for a foul call against Oregon.

"There was a man open," Weber quipped later. "He was making an outlet pass."

As Illinois rolled to the Final Four, it was easier for Weber to laugh at such antics. And it was easier for Smith to avoid them. He could laugh, too, at the way he became a lightning rod for criticism. At the beginning of the season, he told reporters, "As long as we're winning, I can be the butt of a few jokes." Yet Weber wasn't always the only one poking fun. Smith polarized fans, too, with some clamoring for him to play more, others wondering why he played at all.

"I read some stuff, and it was like, 'What an ass,'" Smith said. "But then I'd stand around signing old ladies' purses for an hour—which was pretty funny—and that had to say something about how at least some people around here felt about me. It seems like people either love me or they hate me. I don't get a lot of middle ground, which isn't all bad."

Air-Walking Walk-on

Deron Williams worked hard at basketball, and the rewards were obvious: David Stern called his name on NBA draft night. Luther Head used basketball to gain a sort of redemption, a way to start over after mistakes in his past. But it was harder to see what Fred Nkemdi was getting out of his time on the Illini's roster.

Illinois' senior walk-on came to every practice ready to go to work. He banged. He crashed the boards. He fought and clawed and did all he had to do to help make Illinois better. And in his estimation, it cost him about $50,000.

That's about how much Nkemdi paid in student loans for a two-year stay at Illinois, where he transferred after a stay at Morton College in Cicero, Illinois. A product of Riverside-Brookfield High School in North Riverside, Illinois, Nkemdi was an athletic freak. His Illinois teammates spoke in awe when they told the story of the day he walked into the Ubben Basketball Complex wearing jeans, Timberland boots, and a backpack stuffed with books, then stood underneath the basket and—just for fun—sprung up for a one-handed dunk.

But Nkemdi, six foot five with no knack for playing the back-court, was a man with no position in college basketball. Knowing that the game wasn't in his long-term future, he transferred to Illinois with designs on a political science degree and, eventually, law school.

Most walk-ons have a connection. Those who don't, try to make one. They call the coach they want to walk on for, or they have a high school coach do it. They send letters or highlight films or hope word of mouth gets them an in. Fred Nkemdi called one day to ask when tryouts were. Then he showed up, he played hard, and he waited for a call.

"We actually liked that about him," Weber said.

The call was a few days in coming, but Nkemdi called it his favorite moment as an Illinois player. And he took advantage of the opportunity he was given.

"He works as hard as anybody else," Williams said. "Harder than a lot of guys."

Hard work was in Fred's genes. Nkemdi's father, a prince in the African village where he grew up, came to the United States for college. He played football at Michigan State and met Nkemdi's mother there, and their work ethic was instilled in their son early.

So maybe it was no surprise that he turned into a lunch-pail practice player at Illinois, a guy who showed up, punched the clock, and went to work. Nkemdi wasn't playing for the reward.

Still, he got his moment during a 2004-05 season full of them. Late in Illinois' rout of Oregon at the United Center in December, Nkemdi got loose and finished a fast-break with a vicious dunk on a feed from Brown, a play that brought to life a crowd that had seen its share of spectacular dunks over the years.

"I always hope that somebody got him a really good picture of that," Weber said. "What a memory to have, throwing down a dunk like that in Michael Jordan's house. That's a kid who deserves it."

The Rest: Waiting on the Wings

There may come a time when Rich McBride and Brian Randle and Warren Carter are looked at as key players in Illinois basketball history. There might be a day when Calvin Brock and Shaun Pruitt are fondly remembered for their contributions. If that day comes, fans probably will look back at 2004-05 as a formative year for the players in question.

Randle spent it on the bench, watching and learning, especially from Head, and emerging as such a viable vocal leader that Weber would name him a 2005-06 captain a few months after the Final Four.

McBride played an on-court role in 2004-05, though it was limited. A player with a reputation for his accurate shooting, he was limited by injury and the spectacular play of Brown, Head, and Williams. McBride averaged 14.9 minutes per game and shot just 31 percent from three-point range (86 of his 98 field-goal attempts were three-pointers), but he continued to mature defensively. He spent the spring following the season working to get his body in better shape, hoping to become the type of player on an actual court that he is on a virtual one.

"He'll kill you at video games. I think he's one of the creators of *NBA Live 2004*," joked Randle, McBride's closest friend on the team. "He knows everything about everything in that game. Seriously, I think he invented the game. He's on the credits, probably, if you watch closely."

Like McBride, Carter hoped to develop into a more integral part of the team as a sophomore, and like McBride, the lanky Texan had mixed results. He emerged as a dangerous outside shooter— favoring a midrange baseline jumper, he hit 52.5 percent of his shots—and doubled his scoring average from 1.2 as a freshman to 2.4 as a sophomore. It was at times, Carter said, "the hardest year of my life." But Illinois was winning, so he didn't complain about playing time. Instead, he kept the mood light, joking with teammates and laughing with Augustine when their roommates, Smith and Ingram, got into drawn-out conversations about Ingram's electrical engineering courses.

Rich McBride was the only guard off the bench for the Illini in 2004-05. The sophomore spent the season in a shooting slump but had a deadly virtual touch at video game basketball. *Robin Scholz/The News-Gazette*

Brock took a redshirt year, and Pruitt might as well have. He elected not to sit the season out but appeared in 21 games for a total of only 97 minutes, averaging 1.4 points per game on 38.5 percent shooting.

But there were hardly whispers of transfers—or of disappointment. As Illinois rocked its opponents, its young players rolled with the punches, biding their time for another year. And that willingness to wait, the veterans said, helped secure the path to success in 2004-05.

"We never had a lot of guys thinking, 'Okay, now I have to shine. All these other guys are shining, so now it's my turn,'" Brown said. "We all had love for each other. We all knew as long as the team was shining, everything would come to us. It's love, man. It's chemistry."

Melding the Mixture

It's that love for one another, that genuine enjoyment of each other, that the Illini said made mixing so many personalities such an easy task. That, and a solid sense of humor.

"They never took themselves too seriously," Weber said. "I never had to make sure they were having fun. That was one thing you never had to worry about."

Before a game against Indiana, Weber's players were so relaxed that they broke into fits of laughter as the coach was detailing his game plan. Weber didn't get the joke, but he had to make sure his players got his message.

"So I'm sitting there going, 'Okay, we're going to play a game now,'" Weber said. "I'm like, 'You might want to listen to your coach now. Hello?'"

Eventually the Illini tuned in. Then they took the court and jumped ahead of Indiana 20-3 to open the game. Ten days later, before a game at Penn State, Weber stressed to his players not to let up. He told his 25-0 team not to take the Nittany Lions lightly, that Penn State was due to pull an upset, and would have the top-ranked Illini circled on the schedule. Later, during an afternoon shootaround, Weber found his team holding an impromptu three-point shooting contest. From high in the seats at the Bryce Jordan Center.

"I told everybody I was going to make one from the bench, and I did," Brown said.

"Nobody ever could make one from upstairs," Augustine added.

As different as they were, the Illini could be brought together after all. At heart, they were mostly the same: fun-loving kids who enjoyed the game, who had a passion for playing it. After one game at the Assembly Hall, a reporter going to place a tape recorder on the podium at which players sat to conduct interviews accidentally pulled a microphone off the stand and ripped away part of the batting around the table in the process.

"What the..." Luther Head shouted. Then with Richard Pryor-timed quickness he blurted out a mock headline: "Luther Head: Suspended Again, Breaks Microphone."

The whole room broke out in laughter. His teammates did, too. These guys weren't all so different.

4

RAISE THE CURTAIN

As his team prepared to embark on what would become a magical season, Coach Weber had a sense that he had something special in the works. But he wasn't quite sure just how good the Illini could be, and neither were his players. Practices had gone well at the start, but Weber's veterans had tired of drills and scrimmages. Even as Weber put more and more competitive games into practice, his team's mind started to drift. The Illini were ready to play.

A pair of exhibition games were uneventful, and Weber was anxious to get his team on the court against an actual opponent. Illinois opened its 100th season of basketball with a weekend doubleheader, hosting Delaware State on November 19 and Florida A&M on November 21. During a team meeting that week, Weber broke what most coaches considered a cardinal rule in basketball: he told his team to focus on the games in front of it, but he also urged his players to look ahead. On the dry erase board he often used to drive home his points, Weber wrote simply "13-0," encouraging his team to aim for a perfect record in non-conference play. Enter the Big Ten unbeaten, Weber said, and we'll consider the first stage of the season a success.

"I told them it was all set up for us," Weber said. "We had tough games against some good teams, but they were at home or they were at neutral sites. I told them that it was a realistic possibility, and we made that the first goal of the season, to go undefeated in the preseason."

Of course, they didn't say so—at least publicly. Known for his outspoken style, Weber still knew to keep a few things to himself. And so, for fear of giving added motivation to Illinois' opponents, he kept his team's first major goal a secret. It wasn't until after the Illini accomplished the feat—beating Cincinnati in Las Vegas to achieve pre-conference perfection—that Weber's players let the cat out of the bag. In doing so, they pointed out their coach's own imperfection.

"He actually wrote 13-0 on the board, but then he figured out it was actually 14 [non-conference] games," Deron Williams said. "So he changed it and started saying 14-0 [the week before] the Cincinnati game."

Weber knew his team had a shot at running the table against its non-conference schedule. But even he couldn't have known how easy the Illini would make it look.

High Praise

Illinois did what it was supposed to do early on, blasting inferior competition off the court and proving itself worthy of a No. 5 preseason ranking. The Illini blitzed Delaware State by 20, then romped Florida A&M by 31. By the time Illinois reached its third game of the season, it had established itself as an unselfish offensive juggernaut—without having played particularly well. The Illini showed flashes, certainly, making 12 three-pointers against snail-paced Delaware State and scoring 58 first-half points against Florida A&M. But it was early, and Illinois was a long way from its stride.

That didn't stop coaches from piling on praise, however. In its third game of the season, Illinois ripped Oakland (Michigan) 85-54 behind 22 points from Luther Head and 17 from Williams. James Augustine had a quiet night. Dee Brown, too. And the Illini took it easy on the Golden Grizzlies in the second half, outscoring Oakland 38-26 en route to an easy if seemingly unremarkable victory.

At least it seemed unremarkable to most observers. Not so to Oakland coach Dave Kampehe. "For a single night, that's the best team I've ever seen," Kampehe said. "I don't see a weakness." The praise didn't stop there. Kampehe compared the Illini favorably to the Michigan State teams that made three straight Final Fours under Tom Izzo and won the 2000 NCAA championship.

Though Illinois had outscored its first three opponents 263-181, it had hardly faced NCAA tournament-caliber competition. (Oakland would actually make the NCAA tournament—despite compiling more losses than wins during the season—after winning its conference tournament.) Kampehe's comments were the first by an outsider calling the Illini a legitimate title contender. But it was early, and while Illinois was pounding inferior competition, other teams were playing in high-profile preseason events, testing their mettle against other topflight talent.

Three days after the Oakland game, Illinois stepped up a level. The results brought praise from an authority with more insight— and more credibility—than Dave Kampehe.

The Wizard Watches in Wonder

Since the late 1990s, Gonzaga had begun to build a reputation as a college basketball giant-killer, a quiet powerhouse from the West Coast Conference willing to play—and able to beat—anyone, any-where, anytime. The 2004-05 Zags were no different, a team loaded with talent that was built around big man Ronny Turiaf and sopho-more swingman Adam Morrison. They were supposed to give Illinois its first test of the season. But their game on November 27 in Indianapolis was significant for more than just the teams' Top 25 rankings.

It also was Illinois' first appearance in the Wooden Classic, the event named for UCLA coaching legend and Indiana native John Wooden, who made it a point to appear every year at his namesake doubleheader. For Weber, that was a thrill in itself. The Illinois coach has long employed motivational sayings and daily thoughts as part of his coaching routine, and many were borrowed directly from the so-called "Wizard of Westwood," a coach who became famous for his ability to motivate. "Be quick, but don't hurry," Wooden would tell his team, and the mantra would stick with them for life.

"It's an amazing opportunity for players to get to meet him, for him to talk to them," Weber said. "Those are the things you hope they really appreciate over the course of the season."

To hear Wooden address the state of the game, you might think he's an old codger who doesn't appreciate what basketball has become. He had become well known for despising the showmanship that had permeated the sport, and at nearly every opportunity, he took the time to call for the outlaw of the dunk in college hoops.

But what Wooden saw on that November Saturday in Indianapolis took him back. Even he had to pay respect. Illinois dismantled Gonzaga from the opening tip until midway through the second half, when Weber called off the dogs. The Illini put on a clinic from the moment the jump ball was tossed. They moved the ball (to the tune of 24 assists), they clamped down defensively (forcing 19 turnovers), and they shot brilliantly from the outside (tying a school record with 14 three-pointers, 12 of them by Williams, Head and Brown).

Most of all, though, Illinois functioned as a team. The same way Wooden had taught his teams to play. And the best coach in the building took notice.

"It was as impressive a display as I've seen in quite some time," Wooden said, and coming from the legend, that's practically gushing.

"You had to respect that," Brown said. "That's John Wooden. I think everybody would love to accomplish what he's accomplished in this game. I think everybody aspires to that."

The clobbering of Gonzaga in the Wooden Tradition was Illinois' first link to Coach Wooden in 2004-05, but it wasn't the last. Weber met Wooden then, and his players shook the coach's hand and posed with him for a photo after the game. Later in the year, Weber told an ESPN reporter how often he used Woodenisms in his coaching.

"Make every day your masterpiece," Wooden had told the Illini in Indianapolis, and Weber continued to preach that to his team throughout the year. ESPN liked the story. And sideline reporter Erin Andrews told it during a broadcast later in the season. Wooden, apparently, was watching.

"He sent a big box of books and stuff," Weber said. "I used that stuff all year."

Looking Ahead

When Illinois' guards filed into the media room after the Gonzaga win for the postgame press conference, they answered only a few questions about how they'd taken apart the Zags. Instead, most of the questioning surrounded what still lay ahead.

Four days after the Gonzaga game, No. 1-ranked Wake Forest would invade the Assembly Hall as part of the ACC/Big Ten Challenge, and it promised to be one of the most exciting matchups of the pre-conference season in all of college basketball. In Chris Paul and Justin Gray, the Demon Deacons had a backcourt combo that could match up with Illinois' trio. In Eric Williams, Wake had the broad-shouldered banger that the Illini lacked. And while Illinois had been demolishing Gonzaga and a trio of cupcakes, the Deacons had been battle-tested in winning the Preseason NIT in New York, knocking off Arizona in a thriller to claim the title game.

This matchup of No. 5 versus No. 1 would be college basketball's early season game of the year. And the hype machine warmed up even before the horn sounded on the Gonzaga game. The Illinois-Wake game was being billed as the biggest at the Assembly Hall since 1979, when the Illini had last upset the nation's No. 1 team, stunning Magic Johnson and Michigan State on a buzzer-beating jump shot by Eddie Johnson.

"I wanted our guys to look at the game as an opportunity," Weber said. "But I wanted them to keep their heads level."

That wasn't easy. And not just because the Illini couldn't go anywhere in Champaign without hearing about the game. For Brown and Williams, the chatter extended well beyond the student union.

"We had gotten to be real good friends with Chris Paul and Justin Gray," Williams said. "We played with them in the summer at the Michael Jordan camp and a couple of events, and all four of us got to be real tight, so we were all talking about the game."

With half a week to build up, the hype reached a fever pitch. The game was the first non-conference game selected as a "Paint

Roger Powell Jr. and Luther Head prepare to paint the Hall orange for Wake Forest. The Demon Deacons never knew what hit them, as the Illini rolled past them in a 91-73 victory. Powell led the team with 19 points. *Robert K. O'Daniell/The News-Gazette*

The Hall Orange" night at the Assembly Hall in the history of the event, and Head and Roger Powell Jr. posed on the cover of *The News-Gazette* sports page with orange paint cans, rollers and brushes for a story about the big-game atmosphere in Champaign.

Meanwhile, Brown and Williams' cell phones kept working overtime.

"I was calling them up, just having some fun, talking a little bit," Paul said. "It was friendly stuff. We all talked a lot leading up to that game, right before we came down to Champaign. After that, I didn't talk to them for a while."

You can probably guess why.

"Challenge" Is No Contest

There have been remarkable games over the years at the Assembly Hall, games that will live forever in the minds of Illinois fans. There have been nail-biters and buzzer beaters and some of the most thrilling basketball the Big Ten has had to offer. The Wake

Forest game was supposed to be cut from that same cloth, but it wasn't. It wasn't a down-to-wire masterpiece or a game for the ages. But it's not likely to be forgotten. In fact, it will go down in Illinois basketball history as the signature non-conference performance by the 2004-05 Fighting Illini, and the game that made the nation take notice of what Champaign-Urbana already knew: Illinois was for real.

"It's probably my favorite home game of all my four years," Powell said. "We came out and beat No. 1. That was like a statement game, where we sort of told everybody that we were coming out."

It ended up: Illinois 91, Wake Forest 73. Yet it wasn't nearly that close. Brown blew by the Deacons in the open court. Head rained three pointers. Williams played stifling defense. And for 28 of the 40 minutes that December night, Illinois led the nation's No. 1 team by double digits.

But perhaps no player summed up Illinois' dominance more than Powell, who had prayed before the game as he did before each of them, but who admitted to feeling a little something extra in his step that night. Maybe it was the mismatches, Wake Forest without a player on its roster with the strength and agility to keep up with Powell. Maybe it was the adrenaline, the crowd roaring louder with each Illinois basket and chanting "We're No. 1! We're No. 1!" as the Illini pulled away. Maybe it was a simple matter of religious hierarchy.

"The Deacons couldn't stop the Reverend," Powell said.

Whatever the reason, Powell played like a possessed man. He scored 18 points (sinking two three-point attempts, his second and third of the season), grabbed seven rebounds, and looked like the best frontcourt player on the floor in a game that was supposed to be decided by guards. It still was in many ways; Brown and Williams—with an assist from Head—got the better of their buddies from Winston-Salem.

When it ended, even before the crowd noise had ceased ringing in the Hall, the inevitable question was asked: Was that performance enough to elevate the fifth-ranked Illini to the No. 1 spot? Illinois players said—and still say—that they weren't thinking about it at the time.

"I don't know," Brown said after the game. "After that performance, you tell me."

The Deacons told him, loud and clear.

"If I had a vote," Eric Williams said, "I'd vote them No. 1."

Speeding Over the Road Bumps

To get to the top spot, Illinois would first have to beat Arkansas a few days later in Little Rock, Arkansas. To remain at the top, the Illini would have to endure a stretch of four games in seven days that began with that trip south. But the Illini were prepared for it. Weber had seen to that.

A coach's natural inclination might have been to circle the Gonzaga and Wake Forest games on the preseason schedule. Those, after all, would be Illinois' best chances to make waves before the Big Ten season, its best opportunities to catch the eyes of Top 25 voters and make an early impression on the NCAA tournament selection committee. But Weber didn't do that. Instead, even before the season opener, Weber was selling his team on the importance of three other non-conference games: The Arkansas game, the Georgetown game five days later, and the Oregon game in Chicago two days after that. Sprinkled in between Arkansas and Georgetown was a guaranteed win against Chicago State. Weber wasn't talking much about that one.

"I knew that they would be up for the Gonzaga game and the Wake game," Weber said. "But Arkansas, we knew, was dangerous. It was a neutral-site game, but it was in Little Rock, so it was basically a home game [for them]. And then, with three more games in the next week, we figured that would test their focus. So we tried to get them ready for that early, by selling them on the importance of those games."

The sales pitch got a little easier after the Wake Forest win, which put Illinois in position to claim the No. 1 ranking with a win against the Razorbacks. They did that in hard-fought fashion, riding 19 points from Powell and 13 each from Brown and Williams to a 72-60 win that put Illinois atop the Associated Press and ESPN/*USA Today* Coaches polls the following Monday. In

Champaign-Urbana, that set off a frenzy of entrepreneurship. Enterprising T-shirt shops printed "No. 1" shirts that sold like wild, and fans gleefully chanted "We're No. 1" when the Illini took the court for a predictable rout of Chicago State the night the polls were released.

The Illini had been waiting to see the polls released. Their reaction was subdued.

"It was business," Head said. "It was like, 'We're No. 1, so let's stay there.' We didn't dance around or let off balloons or nothing."

Weber had preached to his team that their stay at No. 1 would be short-lived if they embraced it. Instead, he told his team, strive to stay on top. Understand the target on your back and use it as motivation.

Three days after rising to the top of the polls, the Illini defended the No. 1 spot in Washington, D.C., against Georgetown, a once-proud program trying to rebuild under coach John Thompson III, the son of legendary Georgetown coach John Thompson. A tour of the nation's capital would have to wait until the day after the game. Even then, Weber cut the tour short and made it uneventful, fearing his team would be too weary for a weekend game with Oregon. But the Illini provided plenty of sights on their own against the Hoyas.

Trailing early and struggling to find an offensive rhythm, Illinois—buoyed by a surprisingly orange-clad crowd—dominated the second half of the game and pulled away for a 74-59 win. That left only the Oregon game standing between Illinois and a sweep of its grueling first week at No. 1. And Weber wasn't worried about motivating his players for that. The venue, he figured, would handle that for him.

The Illini always seemed to have an extra bounce in their step at the United Center, and the Oregon game would be no exception. The Illini raced in front of the Ducks by 14 at halftime and cruised to an 83-66 win in Chicago. Weber's gamble had paid off: an early focus on Arkansas, Georgetown, and Oregon helped to ensure that his team was motivated for that stretch. And if that wasn't enough, Weber dangled one extra carrot in front of his players.

Deron Williams led the Illini past Missouri for their fifth straight victory in the annual Braggin' Rights game. *Darrell Hoemann/The News-Gazette*

"He told us it was an NBA schedule," Williams said. "He told us if we wanted to play in the league someday, we had to be ready to play stretches like that. That was a great motivator."

The Right to Brag

During his first season at Illinois, Weber had been welcomed to the Braggin' Rights game with a shock to the system. He'd been told upon accepting the Illinois job that the Missouri Tigers were the Illini's biggest non-conference rival, and that beating them would hold special significance to Illinois fans. But he never expected what happened one snowy December morning in 2003, when, as he woke for his morning ritual, he heard his daughters screaming. There was a cat in the Weber's front lawn—hanging from a tree.

"I thought, 'Oh, God, we're so bad that they're hanging cats in trees,'" Weber said of his Illini. "I thought they were sending a message."

They were. But it was a message of encouragement. The cat in question was a stuffed Tiger. During the night, members of the Orange Krush had hung it in Weber's front yard along with signs urging the Illini to "Beat Mizzou." Weber had been initiated.

Weber's second Braggin' Rights game came and went without any hangings, but the Illini would freely admit they came dangerously close to choking. Entering the game 10-0 and riding a four-game winning streak in the series, Illinois charged out to a 15-point halftime lead, then had to hang on to win. If Illinois had lost, "it would've been a disaster," Williams said.

It could've happened. Mizzou big man Linas Kleiza had 25 points to lead the young Tigers' comeback, and when Jason Horton buried a three-pointer with 14 seconds to play, Missouri cut the lead to four points. But the Illini shot 11 for 12 down the stretch at the free throw line to hold on.

A fifth straight win against their archrivals and an 11-0 start should have been enough to guarantee happy holidays for the Illini. But they were Scrooges in postgame interviews, pleased to have won but clearly disappointed with their performance. Weber, too, had been disappointed, and he left the game with dual concerns. First,

Illinois' defense had been porous in the second half, and Weber wondered if his team was committed to defense after a string of blowout wins. And secondly, his Illini had looked tired. There was a long season ahead, and Weber's starters were logging major minutes. He wondered if his team could hold up for the long haul.

Those concerns weren't lessened after Christmas, when it became apparent that Illinois needed to focus its efforts on defense—and even more apparent that the Illini had set a standard unlike any in Illinois basketball history.

"We went out and crushed Longwood," Brown said. "And it was like we played awful."

Fans thought so. The media, too. And the Illini didn't deny, after a 105-79 win against lowly Longwood in which Lancers star Michael Jefferson scored 30 points, that they had some work to do. They would have to change their ways in Sin City.

Vegas, Baby

When Illinois hit The Strip, it had all the makings of a movie scene. College basketball's rock stars were visiting Las Vegas, and the combination seemed almost too glamorous to fathom. The Illini, after all, were the biggest story in college basketball. Off to a 12-0 start, they were media darlings ready to take Vegas by storm. By virtue of home wins against Valparaiso and Longwood, Illinois was in position to win the Las Vegas Holiday Classic with two wins in the desert—first against Northwestern State and then against college basketball's Bad Boys from Cincinnati.

It should've been like something out of Hollywood. Las Vegas had seemed appealing when it appeared on the schedule, a chance to get away from the barren Illinois campus—deserted over the holiday break—and experience the sights and sounds of one of America's most electrifying cities. On paper, it looked like a season highlight. But the moment Illinois' flight touched down, it was clear that Vegas would be less than they'd imagined.

"It rained," Williams said. "Oh my God, it rained. We land in the middle of the desert, and it's raining. And it just kept on raining."

An inch of rain in Las Vegas, Weber said, is like an impassable snowstorm in Chicago. Cars are stopped on the side of the road. Tourists are afraid to drive, and the locals forget how to. Go outside at any hour and Las Vegas is alive. A heavy shower, though, can put it right to bed.

"You couldn't even walk down the street," Williams said. "There was water up to your ankles."

For most tourists, that's hardly a problem. After all, Vegas offers plenty of entertainment for those unable to leave the confines of their hotel. Most of them, anyway.

"If you want to have fun in Vegas, you need to be 21 or have money," James Augustine said. "Most of us weren't 21, and we didn't have any money."

So while Cincinnati players and coaches were spotted living it up into the wee hours of the morning, Weber's team called it quits early. Seniors Nick Smith and Jack Ingram hit the casinos for a few hours at night, but Head didn't have the money to spare. And Powell? Gambling doesn't have much pull for a licensed minister. Most of the rest of the Illini were too young to venture into the casinos.

"I set a 1 a.m. curfew, and I was worried about it," Weber said. "Most of them were in their rooms long before that."

Even the coaching staff steered clear of the trappings of Las Vegas. Former Marine Jimmy Price, the Illinois strength coach, preferred to walk The Strip, or make use of the weight room at Valley High School, the site of the tournament. Weber and his assistants spent most of their free time scouting.

On the team bus after a practice at Valley High, Gary Nottingham looked at the expanse of Vegas and laughed. There were hotels as far as he could see out the dark tinted windows. Nottingham hadn't bet a dime since arriving.

"They don't keep building these casinos," Nottingham said, "because people keep winning."

Bullying the Bullies

With little to distract them from basketball, the Illini made short work of Northwestern State in its first game in Vegas and looked ahead to a Las Vegas Holiday Classic championship matchup against Cincinnati. In the NCAA tournament the year before, the teams had been painted as polar opposites: the Bearcats the rough-and-tumble trash talkers and the Illini, clean and pristine, as gentlemen taken aback by the smack.

In truth, neither team was as black and white as that portrayal would indicate, and even nine months after Illinois' second-round blowout of the Bearcats in 2004, there were disputes as to just what had transpired between the teams in March. Williams said Cincinnati's Eric Hicks told him he was "too pretty to play ball," and several Illinois players claimed that the Bearcats had slapped a sign bearing Illinois' name outside the NCAA tournament locker rooms.

"Absolute crap," Bearcats coach Bob Huggins called it.

But true or not, the allegations had made for an emotionally charged NCAA tournament meeting, and the Las Vegas rematch had almost the same intensity. The Bearcats had been looking forward to the game since long before they left Cincinnati, hoping not only to avenge their NCAA tournament loss, but to validate their 11-0 start. Huggins' team hadn't lost coming into the Illinois game, but a weak schedule had kept the Bearcats in the lower reaches of the Top 25. They wouldn't climb out after the Illinois game.

It became obvious early on, when Brown swiped a lazy Cincinnati inbound pass for a layup-and-foul, that Illinois still had a decided edge in quickness and athleticism. And Williams, though he shot just six-for-15, had the look of a lottery pick, controlling the game and shutting down six-foot-eight Cincinnati forward Armein Kirkland, who shot one-for-eight. What the game lacked in entertainment value—Illinois won 67-45 and was rarely threatened—it made up for in rich irony. By early in the second half, Cincinnati had proven to be paper 'Cats.

"They were crying to the refs for fouls," Brown said. "They said we were too physical."

In the locker room afterward, Weber congratulated his team for meeting the first of its preseason goals. The Illini were entering the Big Ten season 14-0 and looking every bit like the nation's most dominant team.

"We can't let this be the end," Weber told his players. "This has to be a start."

5

THE COACHES

t is safe to call Bruce Weber "old school." He sees the term as a compliment. This, after all, is a man who came up in a different era of the Big Ten, a time when coaches' personalities overwhelmed the league landscape. Weber was a longtime assistant for noted straight-talker Gene Keady in an age when characters like Indiana's Bob Knight, Michigan State's Jud Heathcote, and Illinois' Lou Henson worked the sidelines and held court in the press rooms, discussing their jobs in high style. So it should be no surprise that Weber, right from the start, knew only one way to be: frank.

My first memories of dealing with Weber came at the Las Vegas Invitational in 2001, which was my first year on the Illinois beat. Weber, then the coach at Southern Illinois, had brought his team to Las Vegas with one goal: To reach the finals of the Thanksgiving tournament and play Illinois, which at the time was ranked second in the nation.

"We've been talking about it since the summer," Weber said upon his arrival to the desert. "We just hope Illinois gets there, too."

That comment rubbed Bill Self the wrong way. But it wasn't the first time Weber had rankled a coach for saying what was on his mind, and it wouldn't be the last. I would come to find out over the next few years that there's no filter in Bruce Weber's head. "If I don't lie," he likes to say, "I don't have to remember what I said."

He probably doesn't remember a word of what he said that afternoon in Vegas, but I remember it pretty vividly. I remember liking Weber. I remember everyone else on the Illinois beat liking him, too. And after his Salukis almost beat the Illini—a Sean Harrington three-pointer that hit the front of the rim and rolled over and through the net prevented the monster upset—I remember thinking this guy had something going for him.

"He could be a big-time coach," I told a friend. "But he's so honest around the media, I doubt anybody will ever hire him." (I was glad to be wrong.)

Covering a major coaching search at Illinois is like swimming in mud. It requires a lot of effort and produces very little progress. So in 2002, when I next talked to Weber, I didn't expect the conversation to prove very fruitful. Illinois athletic director Ron Guenther, after all, is notorious for silencing job candidates. He doesn't want leaks in the press. He wants to conduct a one-man search and fill his opening, and he'd just as soon the press and public find out who he selected when he introduces his man at a press conference on campus. So when I called Weber's office at Southern Illinois two days after Self officially took the Kansas job, I expected a secretary to answer. I expected to be told "Coach Weber is unavailable." Instead, the voice that answered was—unmistakably—Weber's.

"I want that job," he went on to tell me. "I know there's an athletic director there who doesn't want me to talk about this, but I don't know any other way to be with you but honest. I want the job."

And he was pretty sure he was going to get it. Weber had read Guenther's comments in the newspapers that day. He knew that Guenther—clearly feeling burned by losing Lon Kruger to the NBA and Self to another college program in the span of three years—was looking for a loyal coach—a guy who could and would stay put. Guenther wanted a coach who was a proven winner at the Division I level.

"If he was being honest," Weber told friends then, "I'm going to get that job."

He made no such proclamation on the phone that day. But right away, a part of me was selfishly rooting for Weber. He seemed like he'd be a fun coach to cover. As a reporter, candor and accessibility are what you're looking for in a coach. Weber brought both to the table—by the truckload. He wasn't the only coach whom I spoke with in the days after Self left, but he was the most candid. He was the most refreshing. He was the only one who answered his own phone in atypical fashion for a coach.

More than hope, I had a hunch, a feeling that Weber was Guenther's man. I don't know how close Guenther ever got to hiring someone else. He certainly isn't going to say. I do know that when a source confirmed for me that Weber was the man, I wasn't surprised. I was just hoping he wouldn't change as a person. Big-time college basketball has a way of doing that to a guy, making him politically correct, conservative, boring. I didn't want Bruce Weber to quit talking.

In retrospect, it's hilarious that I even considered the possibility. By now, Weber's frankness is infamous. One example stands out: the "funeral" that Weber staged for Self during his first season at Illinois, when he wore all black and told his players that their former coach was gone and that it was time to get over it. But his friends know that he's more than just an outrageous sound bite waiting to happen. Ask and they'll tell you that he's also among the hardest-working men in his profession.

Weber inherited most of the players who made the run to the 2004-05 Final Four. But his success coaching them was no accident.

A Day in the Life

During the basketball season, a typical Bruce Weber day begins at about 6:45 a.m., when he gets up—as he always has—to help get his daughters ready for school. There's less to do now, as his girls are in their teens and one is already off to college, but he helps with breakfast. He eats with them before they leave, taking advantage of a rare moment during the day to be with his girls.

When the kids are out the door, Weber and his wife, Megan, leave too. They take the dogs—Daisy and Penny—for their daily walk. For Weber, it's vital, stress-free exercise. And more.

"It's really one of the only times we get to talk, Megan and I," Weber said. "So we value that time. We just talk about our days, talk

Coach Bruce Weber oversees practice at the Ubben Basketball Complex. A typical Illini practice runs well over two hours, but the coaching staff's preparation for each practice extends far beyond that. *AP/WWP*

about the kids, talk about whatever. Usually not basketball. It's our time."

After that, it's off to the office. Because he takes family time in the morning, Weber's rarely in the office before 8 a.m. But once he's there, he sets up camp. He often eats lunch at his desk. He never goes a day without meeting with his staff, usually just before practice, but sometimes more than once. Often, there are media responsibilities to attend to. On Mondays during the conference season, Weber joins the rest of the Big Ten coaches on a media conference call, each coach fielding questions from out-of-town reporters for about 10 minutes. He has a press conference for local media afterward. He also has a regular radio-show call-in to Chicago on Thursdays. And during 2004-05, he fielded a dozen calls a day seeking interviews.

"I gave my cell phone number to too many people," Weber said. "Radio people, some writers. Now they've all got it, and they don't even go through Kent (Brown, Illinois' sports information director). They just call me up."

If those were the only phone calls Weber had during the day, he'd still be swamped. But there are coaches calling as well—and wannabe coaches looking for jobs. There are friends and family. Often, there are recruits to call. There are meetings with players. And then there's the small matter of practice, every day at or around 3 p.m.

"Probably the biggest difference between being [at Illinois] and being at Southern Illinois are the demands on [my] time," Weber said. "There have been times where I'm going in so many directions that I feel like I'm not focusing on practice and on our players. That's why I'm here."

Weber begins practice with a light drill—with no contact—such as shooting or some layups. Then there's a team meeting in front of a dry erase board where Weber drives home the "thought of the day," usually a phrase or saying intended to draw his team's attention. A typical practice in the preseason—the weeks between October 15 and the Illini's first game in November—runs close to three hours, maybe more. During the season, practices are shorter: around two hours, typically. Practices are intense and competitive, and Weber is no casual observer. He's active. To illustrate a defensive drill, he'll jump in the mix and slide his feet. When it's time to work on rebounding, he's the one firing up the missed jump shots.

"I've always said the best head coaches work like assistants," Illinois assistant Jay Price said. "Tom Izzo works like an assistant. Coach Weber works like an assistant."

That means staying at the Ubben Basketball Complex until at least 6 p.m., often later. If he needs to, Weber will sneak away early to pick up one of his daughters from an after-school activity. But once he gets home, his work day isn't over. Not even close.

"We have dinner at 7:30," Weber said. "Or 8 or 9 or 10. It varies."

There's family time then, a chance to chat with Megan and the kids, or to help with homework, if it's needed. And then, when everyone goes to bed, Bruce Weber goes back to work. He watches film. He jots his thoughts down on paper. He might have a beer. Late at night, when he thinks of something he wants to make sure not to forget, he'll call an assistant's office phone and leave a message, a habit he's had for years.

"I used to stay up until 2:30 in the morning," Weber said. "Now I'm more of a 1:30 guy."

On a typical day, that is. On a game night? Forget it.

"I'm up until three, no matter what," he said. "Win, lose, whatever. I'm too wired. I'm thinking too much about the game. I can't stop. So I'm up until three, if I'm lucky. Sometimes later. And then I sleep a few hours and start all over again."

Family Affair

When Weber arrived at Illinois, he hired Price from Purdue to fill one assistant coaching position. He brought Chris Lowery with him from Southern Illinois to fill the other. Lowery then left before the start of the 2004-05 season to take the head coaching job at Southern, and Weber brought another Purdue assistant, Tracy Webster, into the fold. His third assistant was inherited.

Wayne McClain was something of a coaching legend in Illinois, a three-time state title winner at Peoria Manual High School whose best players—his son, Sergio, Marcus Griffin, and Frank Williams—had gone on to form the core of Self's first team at Illinois. McClain was hired the year after Sergio and Griffin had left the program, and though some joked that he'd been brought on board solely to decipher the enigma that was Frank Williams, McClain had proven a valuable asset.

When Self left for Kansas, McClain decided he'd like to stay put. "Illinois is home—it's where my roots are," he said. McClain was particularly helpful during a difficult transition period after Self had left and Weber had been hired. Players were hurt by the transition. Some—Dee Brown included—had publicly considered transferring. McClain was a steadying influence at that time, and that had sped up the bonding process with Weber, Lowery, and Price. By the time Webster joined the staff, McClain was a part of the family. And that's perhaps the best way to describe a Weber staff.

"They really are your basketball family," Weber said. "Family is an important thing to us. I encourage my coaches, when they need to, to get out and spend time with their kids. I was an assistant a long time. I know what it's like. I want these guys to have lives."

He also expects them to work. And to do the job right.

"He's sort of a perfectionist," said Matt McCumber, Illinois' head manager in 2004-05 and an aspiring coach himself. "Not in a bad way. But if you're doing something for a basketball camp, he'll call you 10, 12 times to remind you or make sure you did it."

Weber has a hand in everything that goes on at the Illinois basketball office, a practice that dates back to his jack-of-all-trades role as an 18-year assistant. He makes calls about scheduling. He is hands-on at his basketball camps. He leaves no figurative stone unturned.

"That's why he's out there loading the bus," Price said. "He really does work like an assistant."

Not that it eases the load on his staff. Being a basketball coach at a program like Illinois is a full-time job—and then some. You'll burn the midnight oil. You'll work, sometimes, from dawn to dusk—and well beyond. And if you know what you're doing, you'll get into more than your share of arguments.

"When I was an assistant, I could speak my mind," Weber said. "Coach [Gene] Keady wanted us to do that. He didn't always listen, but we could always give our input."

It's the same at Illinois. When McClain spots a defensive lapse, he's free to jump the offending player ("Brian Randle!," he'll shout, "This isn't Peoria Notre Dame! That won't work here!"). If Webster or Price have a suggestion about how to guard an inbound pass, they are expected to speak up.

"There are times when he does things that are just ridiculous, just to test us," Price said. "He just wants to see if we'll speak up."

Other times Weber is dead serious, but he still invites debate.

"We have it out," Weber said. "If you could hear some of our meetings. They're brutal. We're yelling and screaming, and it's, 'We've got to do it this way!' or 'We've got to do it that way!' That's what I like. I think that's good coaching. But that's easy for me to say, because ultimately, I get the last word."

The Personalities

If Weber has a right-hand man, it's Price, who by the end of 2004-05 had become Illinois' most likely candidate to move to a head coaching position. If the players have a go-to guy, it's McClain, the father figure of the group. The older brother role falls to Webster, the most recent—and perhaps best—college player on the staff. He has been where Illinois' players are, as a standout guard at Wisconsin.

"It's a good mix," Weber said. "I never really thought of it until somebody pointed it out, but I'm an old white guy, and Jay is kind of a young white guy, and Wayne's an older black guy and first Chris and now Tracy are young black guys. Not that [race and age] matter, but it shows you balance. That's what you want on a staff. Different people. Different personalities."

But all with one common thread. Like the players who play for them, Illinois' coaches never seem to take themselves too seriously.

"We have fun," Webster said. "We're all just blessed to be alive. We're enjoying our time."

Luther Head is congratulated by assistant coach Wayne McClain after the Illini advanced to the Final Four. McClain serves as a father figure to the team, and his contributions during Bruce Weber's transitional first season at Illinois were especially helpful. *Jonathan Daniel/Getty Images*

So Webster would stay after practice, sometimes for a half-hour or more, accepting Dee Brown's trick-shot challenges. The two would toss underhanded three-pointers with a bowler's motion, or pitch up 23-foot bank shots behind their backs. When Webster would launch an airball, he'd get an earful. But even Brown's put-downs came tinted with respect.

"I would listen to him anyway, because he's my coach," Brown said. "But that guy has been here before. He's been a point guard in this league at Wisconsin. So when he talks, you want to listen."

The same is true of McClain, whom Weber has often said the players turn to when they need a father figure to guide them. Tough but caring, McClain is brutal on players during practice, taunting them for poor effort or bad shot selection. He's also quick to encourage a player who's down or mired in a slump.

"If there's one good thing I could say about myself, it's that I know people," McClain said. "I know kids. Coaching high school, coaching at this level, you don't do that for a long time without getting to know kids."

Price is perhaps the most polished of the three, the most ready to handle the media requirements that come with being a head coach. He's quick, too, with quips. When James Augustine strolled to the podium at Illinois' postseason banquet to accept an award, Price brought down the room saying, "Careful James—you'll probably get called for two or three fouls on the way up here," a reference to Augustine's foul trouble in the NCAA title game against North Carolina.

A feel for people, a sense of comic timing, a hard-nosed work ethic: These are things Illinois' assistant coaches have in common. And sometimes there's little else. There doesn't need to be.

"Coach Weber doesn't want to have the same guys around him," Price said. "He doesn't want yes-men. He wants different personalities, different people who stand up to him. That's why this works."

The Scouts

Weber has known Gary Nottingham for more than 20 years, and it's hard to imagine how many stories Nottingham has told him in that span of time. Nottingham has thousands of them from his days in West Virginia, tales of the road and of recruiting, homespun stories that come complete with the exaggeration time tends to add.

It's ironic that these days, Nottingham's primary responsibilities as administrative assistant often revolve around film. He's doing digital work, but he's an old-school analog guy. But he's no old-timer. Chances are he stays up later than your teenager.

"I can't tell you how many nights we've been over here until two in the morning," Nottingham said, surveying the cluttered film room that is the hub of Illinois' advanced scouting. Nottingham and Illinois' managers are charged with sorting through film and creating scouting tapes for Illini players, a task that can be arduous. But

Nottingham fills the hours with those stories. And if they don't make the time move any faster, they at least make it more bearable.

But be warned: "Don't listen to a word," joked McClain, who calls Nottingham "The Sheriff." "He has no idea what he's talking about." Nottingham knows basketball, though. And he knows his way around a film room, if not a computer. Most of the film work Illinois does these days is done with digital film, a faster, more efficient method than Nottingham used in his early coaching days. That doesn't mean he's become comfortable with it.

"The managers are very computer literate," Nottingham said. "If it was up to me to figure out a computer, we'd never get any of this done."

The Support Staff: Unsung Heroes

Weber didn't make a shot in 2004-05. He didn't grab a rebound. And he was unfailing in his praise of the guys who did. Credit the players, he would say—but not just the players. As a longtime assistant, Weber is keenly aware of how many people have to do their jobs in order for a basketball program to run smoothly. At every opportunity, Weber thanked his secretary, Cindy Butkovich, for keeping the basketball office on track. His praise for former trainer Rod Cardinal—who was the key to the 2004-05 centennial celebration, spending more than a year in preparation for the event—was constant. And Weber was quick to credit Cardinal's successor, Al Martindale, for the part he played at the NCAA tournament in getting Luther Head ready to play during the Regional weekend in Rosemont.

Even on Weber's much-appreciated staff, though, there are unsung heroes. Like Illinois' managers, who log long hours with no monetary reward, doing duties that are as unglamorous as they are critical.

"Now that," Weber said, "is a thankless job."

But it's not without its perks. Matt McCumber grew up idolizing Illinois basketball players. A three-sport high school athlete in nearby Tuscola, he came to the U of I as a freshman with no hope of competing in Division I sports, but still wanting to be a part of the experience nonetheless. He became a manager his freshman year, and four years later, in 2004-05, he was set to graduate and—he hoped—begin his coaching career.

"It's been the best experience of my life," he said.

An odd sentiment, you might think, for a guy who started out fetching Gatorade and wiping wet spots off the court. But McCumber had, over the course of four years, met people (like Bill Murray) and been places (like Europe) he never dreamed of while living in Tuscola. During his senior year, as Illinois prepared to play Northwestern State in Las Vegas, McCumber stayed at the casino in the Paris Hotel into the wee hours. Unlike the players, the managers were free to roam the strip after curfew. As a result, he now has a story that he can tell forever. As he strolled to the hotel elevator at about 3 a.m., he turned to look at one of the diehards who'd outlasted him that night: Cincinnati coach Bob Huggins.

The managers were part of the Illinois basketball family, another cog in the Illini basketball machine. And whether it was attributable to staff chemistry or simply to a coach who never ran out of gas, that machine kept running smoothly in 2004-05.

"I remember talking as a staff at the beginning of the year, and we had a sense that things were looking good, that we could do something special," Weber said. "I don't think any of us knew how good."

6

KEEPING THE STREAK ALIVE

The Big Ten had become known in recent years for its competitive balance, but as league play opened in 2005, conference coaches were wondering out loud whether that balance might have shifted. In years past, a 13-3 record in conference play typically had been enough to be in the hunt for the Big Ten title. But with the Illini entering conference play 14-0, there was some question as to whether that mark would cut it in 2004-05.

"I always think three losses will put you right there," Michigan State coach Tom Izzo said as conference play dawned. "With Illinois playing the way they are, I might have to rethink that this year."

Izzo was an authority on the subject. His 2000 NCAA title team had lost its first Big Ten game and then ran the table to finish 15-1, running away with the league championship. After the way Illinois had dominated its non-conference competition, fans and media alike were asking if the Illini might do the Spartans one better and go undefeated in Big Ten play. But Weber, who had now famously scrawled that "14-0" on the dry-erase board in the pre-conference season, wasn't setting any similar bar for the conference season. In team meetings, he talked about defending the 2004 Big Ten title, the first the school had won outright since 1952.

The focus had expanded to include bigger prizes. For years, Illinois had broken its huddles after practice by shouting "1, 2, 3 ... Big Ten champs!" stating the conference crown as a goal. By early in the 2004-05 season, Dee Brown and company had upped the ante.

Brown still would shout, "1, 2, 3," and his teammates would respond "Big Ten champs!" But he'd follow with, "4, 5, 6," followed by a group response of "National champs!" And the Illini capped off the give and take with Brown yelling, "7, 8, 9," before his teammates shouted "Family!"

But while the Illini weren't bashful about these team goals, they mostly clammed up when talk turned to going undefeated—even in the Big Ten. It wasn't a goal, the players said. A Big Ten title and a national championship were all that mattered.

"Goals should be something you can actually achieve," James Augustine said.

In January, with the Big Ten season just beginning, it seemed like the right philosophy. Before the conference season ended, though, the undefeated talk would resurface. And considering the way the Illini dominated the conference, it wouldn't seem so far-fetched.

Homecoming, Part 1

Illinois entered conference play on a roll unlike any team in the nation, but the Illini's first Big Ten opponent was one of the nation's most surprising teams. Thad Matta brought Ohio State to the Assembly Hall on January 5, and though it was his first trip into the building as a head coach, the surroundings were quite familiar. As a high school star in Hoopeston, Illinois—less than an hour from Champaign—Matta had led his team to the boys' state tournament, held then at the Assembly Hall.

"I just remember the feeling of playing in that building where so many great Illinois players had played," Matta said. "It gave [me] a real sense of the history of Illinois basketball."

But it hadn't given Matta the chills. Hoopeston was a town divided, centrally located between a triangle of Big Ten schools, and though Matta held no ill will toward the Illini, he'd been more enamored by Indiana and Purdue while growing up. Still, his ties to Central Illinois were strong, and his success at Butler and Xavier had made him a popular choice among some Illini fans to succeed Bill Self when he left for Kansas. Of course, Weber had gotten the job,

James Augustine helped Illinois get its Big Ten campaign off on the right foot with 21 points and 10 rebounds in the Illini's 84-65 win over Ohio State. *Robin Scholz/The News-Gazette*

and by the time Matta brought his team to his home state, Weber could have won a mayoral election in a landslide.

Still, it was apparent to anyone at the Hall that night that Matta was doing something right at Ohio State. The specter of NCAA probation hung over the program, and the Buckeyes had banned themselves from NCAA tournament play after an internal investigation into recruiting violations committed during fired coach Jim O'Brien's tenure. The team that opened conference play against Illinois, though, was a different one than O'Brien had coached the year before. Most of the personnel was the same, but Matta's team had an energy, an intensity that had been lacking in the final year of O'Brien's successful run in Columbus. It showed early against the Illini. Ohio State made seven first-half three-pointers and trailed the nation's No. 1 team by only six points at halftime.

"They came out and played hard," Brown said. "That's what it's like when you're No. 1. You get everybody's best shot."

Ultimately, even Ohio State's best shot wasn't good enough. Weber made some halftime adjustments, and the Buckeyes shot three for 10 from three-point range in the second half as the Illini pulled away to an 84-65 blowout.

"They're a good team," Weber said afterward of Ohio State. Unlike many observers, he wasn't surprised by the Buckeyes. He had picked them as a dark horse in the league the year before, and with a roster that was essentially the same but with more experience, he had expected improvement. "I can guarantee you, it's not going to be easy to go to their place at the end of the year and win."

Illinois would soon find it wouldn't be easy to win anywhere.

Homecoming, Part 2

When you're No. 1, everyone wants to take you down. When you're No. 1 and undefeated, the desire is that much more intense. And when underdog players take a personal stake in the game, it's a recipe for an upset.

Purdue was that sort of team, a struggling squad that was scuffling through Gene Keady's last season as coach, a team in need of a validating win, a magic moment in a farewell season that had been devoid of them. And the Boilermakers knew that they could give their coach no better gift than a win against Weber, his longtime protégé.

Purdue had, with much fanfare, brought in Southern Illinois head coach Matt Painter—a former Weber assistant at the Carbondale school and onetime Boilermaker player—to serve as Keady's associate coach for a year before taking over as head coach in 2005-06. It wasn't the first time Purdue had made such an offer. Weber, in fact, had been asked to return to West Lafayette early in his stay at Southern Illinois. Friends in the Purdue athletic department had told Weber, when he was Keady's assistant, to find a head coaching job and make himself a more viable candidate for the Boilers' job when Keady retired. Soon after he left, he got an offer to return. Unlike in Painter's case, however, there had been a catch.

"They didn't know when Coach was going to retire," Weber said. "So the option was to come back without knowing for sure if I would have the job in a year or two years or three. I couldn't do that. I couldn't leave Southern for that."

So Weber stayed put. And when he took the Illinois job, he broke the hearts of Purdue fans who'd longed to see him return to Mackey Arena on the home sideline. On recruiting trips to Indiana, Purdue fans would approach him and offer congratulations with a caveat. "I hate to say this," a Boiler fan once told Weber, "but you're doing a great job there."

That sort of mixed emotion about Weber—and a mixed crowd in Mackey Arena, packed with thousands of Illinois fans—only added to the intensity the hungry Boilermakers already possessed going into the teams' January 8 meeting. For a while, Purdue fans thought that they might send the folks in orange home feeling blue. Their team got off to a blazing start and led 39-33 at halftime, the first team all season to take a lead into the locker room against the Illini.

Yet Weber didn't appear worried, and it was clear why: Purdue had taken its best shot, and Illinois had plenty more gas left in the tank. Weber ripped his team at halftime, and the Illini in turn ripped Purdue, outscoring the Boilermakers 35-20 in the second half of a 68-59 win, notable mostly for the debut of Brown's infamous jersey tug. Purdue fans had ridden Brown most of the first half. But by the time the game ended, Brown had 14 points and four three-pointers, and he played to the Illini crowd.

"I just couldn't keep it in. I was so excited," Brown said of popping his jersey. "It was just my way of telling our fans, 'Thanks for coming out. This is Illinois basketball.'"

Big Wins, Little Problem

If the Purdue game made anything apparent, it was that the standard that the Illini had set was mile-high. A nine-point win on the road against a conference opponent is supposed to be—by most any standard—an impressive showing. But after Illinois trailed the Boilermakers for virtually the entire first half, fans and analysts began to wonder if there were chinks in the Illini armor.

Weber didn't worry. Instead, he raised the bar on his team. With lowly Penn State coming to the Assembly Hall, he pulled out a motivational ploy he'd used in the preseason to great effect: He told his team to maul the Nittany Lions. Not just beat them, but blow them out.

"It's the first time in my career that I've actually told [a team] before games if they don't win by 30, it's disappointing," Weber said. "Most of the time you don't say that, but I already know they're mentally complacent, so I'm trying to push them and give them a challenge."

Fans cringed when Weber not only employed the tactic, but told the media about it. It sounded arrogant, some worried. It would fire up opposing teams and make Weber look classless. But Weber clearly meant no harm. Penn State's coach, Ed DeChellis, had long been a friend of Weber's. And after the Illini blasted Penn State 90-64 at the Hall, Weber apologized to his friend for playing his starters so many minutes.

"We just don't have a lot of depth in our backcourt," Weber said. "We've got to play somebody."

Weber's players, meanwhile, didn't discourage his practice of preaching blowouts. Quite the contrary, they said, it kept them focused, kept their minds from wandering when they built big leads.

Luther Head scored a team-best 19 points in Illinois' 90-64 win over Penn State at the Assembly Hall. Head was the Illini's most consistent scorer during the season, leading the team in scoring seven times during the Big Ten season and 16 times overall. *Robert K. O'Daniell/The News-Gazette*

"Coach Self was like, 'A win is a win,' but Coach Weber is a little more up front," Brown said. "He's like, 'If you play Illinois basketball, you should win big,' and if it doesn't happen, then you probably came out lackadaisical."

Sticks and Stones, Etc.

When Weber's blowout talk didn't rally the troops, an outside influence often did the trick. When Illinois traveled to Northwestern on January 15, the Illini already were fired up by their loss in Evanston the season before, only the Wildcats' first win against Illinois in 10 tries. But Northwestern students added fuel to the fire that Saturday afternoon, and Cats coach Bill Carmody probably wished they hadn't. As Illinois warmed up, fans taunted players and support staff, and no one took a more vicious verbal beating than manager Brandon Smith. Smith, a Chicago kid who shared an apartment with Brown and Luther Head, was serenaded with chants of "Fat Albert" and bombarded with food scraps, including pizza crust.

"It was disrespectful," said Head. The attacks on his friend only served to strengthen Head's determination. He had been terrorized the year before by the Wildcat student section. Students had held up driver's licenses and made "handcuffed" gestures to Head, who at the time was playing his first game back after a suspension for driving on a suspended license. One fan even brought a sign with a list of items stolen from an apartment during a break-in that Head had been accused of participating in.

With so much motivation, it was no surprise that Head was fired up for his return to Evanston. He scored 26 points as Illinois rolled 78-66 and was never seriously threatened. The win moved the Illini to 18-0—the best start in school history. That wasn't Head's only cause for celebration, though. After a nifty reverse lay-up late in the game, Head glared back at the Northwestern students, and then his face shifted to a wide smile. On the sideline, Brandon Smith was smiling, too.

"The whole thing with their students was just fun," Weber said, but the coach equated it with a game the year before, when

Maryland-Eastern Shore players had talked trash during warmups before getting run out of the Assembly Hall.

"It's like, 'God, that's not very smart,'" Weber said. "You're already going to get beat."

Hawkeye Bull's-Eye

Before the season, I asked Nick Smith about Illinois' goals for the 2004-05 season, and talk eventually turned to the thought of winning at Wisconsin. The Badgers hadn't lost a Big Ten game at the Kohl Center under Bo Ryan, and their homecourt winning streak would stretch well into the 30s by the time Illinois was set to visit on January 25.

"If we could win there, that would be sweet," Smith said before the season. "... That would just about make the season."

The Illini's list of goals had since expanded, but thoughts of the Wisconsin game permeated the program for weeks before the teams met, particularly after the Badgers pulled a miracle comeback against Michigan State to keep the streak alive and prevent the Spartans from snatching streak-snapping headlines.

Illinois was ready for the Badgers early. The only problem was that the Illini had games to play before they visited Madison. Maybe that distraction had an impact on Illinois' game against Iowa on January 20. Or maybe Illinois was just flat. Or maybe Iowa guard Pierre Pierce just put the Hawkeyes on his shoulders with the intent to do the unthinkable. Whatever the case, Iowa almost did it. On a frigid night in January, Illinois' most hated Big Ten rival almost won at the Assembly Hall. Almost.

The game didn't go according to an upset script. Though they weren't at their absolute best, the Illini still shot 46 percent in the first half and led by nine points heading into the locker room. But Pierce took over in the second half, and the Hawkeyes rallied as Illinois got sloppy and took questionable shots. When Roger Powell Jr. launched his third three-pointer of the game—he missed all three—Weber quipped, "I wanted to reach out and block it."

Iowa scored seven of the last eight points in regulation, and when Brown missed one of two free throws in the closing seconds,

Steve Alford's team had a chance to win. Instead of taking a three-pointer—Pierce had made two as part of a 22-point effort, and Iowa finished with eight—the Hawks went to Greg Brunner, whose driving lay-up tied the game at 65 and sent it to overtime. In the extra period, Illinois scored only one field goal, a Luther Head lay-up. But they converted six free throws and managed to hold on by limiting Iowa to just three points in overtime.

Five days separated the Iowa game from the Wisconsin trip, and Weber, worried about his team's mental state, shut off media access during that period. After the Iowa game, though, it was clear that the players were disgusted.

"People were saying we needed to lose a game," Head said. "Well, I guess you can take this one as a loss."

Getting Badgered

Practices leading up to the Wisconsin game were some of the most intense of the season. Still upset with the way they'd played against Iowa—and motivated not only to keep their unbeaten streak alive, but to end Wisconsin's homecourt dominance—the Illini were vicious and vocal. Miss a defensive assignment and you were getting a tongue-lashing. Make an ill-advised pass, and there would be hell to pay.

"You could tell they had a little something extra," Illinois assistant Jay Price said. "They were fired up."

And with good reason. Though Iowa was the Big Ten team that Illini fans most despised, the Hawkeyes hadn't matched Illinois' recent success. And though Michigan State was a perennial threat to win the Big Ten, the Illini and Spartans had a friendly rivalry. They joked with each other before games and hung out together at Big Ten media days.

With Wisconsin it was different. The Badgers had become a consistent Big Ten force under Bo Ryan, and their crowning moment had come at Illinois' expense. When Brown, Williams, and Augustine were freshmen, they had lost a road game at Wisconsin that decided the Big Ten title. Brown had committed the foul on the Badgers' Devin Harris that led to a clinching free throw. That game had long been a source of private frustration, more for Brown than for anyone.

"If I did what I was supposed to do, I might have another ring," Brown told me once. "Wisconsin isn't my favorite school in the Big Ten. I don't really like any of 'em, but Wisconsin, they're just not my favorite."

With that pain as a backdrop, Illinois yearned to burn the Badgers at Kohl. So Weber wasn't surprised when his players were dialed in for practices, nor when they were focused at the shootaround the day before the game. And when Weber stood before his team on game night in the expansive Kohl Center locker room, he didn't have to deliver a motivational speech. It was Xs and Os. All business.

Weber's only button-pushing tactic was to scribble a single word across the dry erase board on which he'd diagrammed that night's matchups: "Believe."

A Limber Jack

The Fighting Illini believed, and early on it showed. They raced out to an early lead against the Badgers, controlling the game and the tempo and forcing Ryan into an early timeout. But Wisconsin hadn't won 38 consecutive games at home by getting rattled, and as the game wore on, the Badgers whittled away at the Illini lead. At halftime, Wisconsin trailed by only two, 35-33, and it looked as though the second half might belong to the Badgers.

The second half looked at times like a repeat of Wisconsin's blowout win against the Illini the year before at the Kohl Center, a game in which Illinois lost its cool as the Badgers got hot. Forgetting how they had built a lead in the first place, the Illini gave up easy baskets in transition. They failed to close out on Wisconsin's shooters from three-point range. And they made easy plays look difficult, tossing passes out of bounds and committing unforced turnovers. Midway through the half, Wisconsin led by eight points. Then, an unlikely pair of heroes emerged.

The first never took a shot. Sophomore Brian Randle, dressed as always in street clothes, sat at the end of the bench. His surgical-

The key to Illinois' victory over Wisconsin at the Kohl Center was the play of Jack Ingram. A pair of three-pointers by Ingram capped a 13-2 Illini run late in the game. *Heather Coit/The News-Gazette*

ly repaired left hand was still sore, and his blood pressure was soaring. Randle hadn't played a minute all season, and he wouldn't get into a game, electing to take a medical redshirt. That didn't mean he couldn't get involved, though. During a timeout, he ripped into his teammates, berating them for making careless plays and letting the lead slip away. A few Illini, none too happy to be attacked by a player who hadn't played a meaningful game in 10 months, snapped back.

"I don't know how the players took it," Weber said. "But to [the coaches], it was great."

It was that moment, Weber would say the following summer, that made him realize that Randle could develop into a leader. For many, it was a surprising choice when Weber named Randle a co-captain on the 2005-06 squad (along with the more experienced Brown and Augustine). To Weber, Randle had proven himself an emotional leader during his redshirt season without ever playing a game.

Randle's motivational speech, though, couldn't get the Illini back in the game. For that, they turned to another unlikely source. It wasn't uncommon on winter nights to see Jack Ingram stay after practice and drain a flurry of three-pointers. He'd make 20 out of 25 sometimes, popping the net just so. Once, during a morning practice, Ingram bailed his team out on consecutive possessions during a 30-second drill in which the object was to shut down your opposition for 30 consecutive seconds. Twice that morning, Ingram beat the buzzer with long three-pointers to keep his team from losing.

Ryan didn't know that Ingram was a shooter. The Badger players didn't know. Nor did the 17,142 fans packed into the Kohl Center. During a furious rally the Illini twice found Ingram open for a three-point attempt. There was no gasp from the Wisconsin crowd, no fear that the muscle-bound six-foot-10 engineering student might sink the shots that ultimately did in the Badgers.

"They were just good shots," Ingram said. "I was open, and they were good shots. The guys got me the ball. You get shots like those, you have to take them."

Ingram did, twice. Swish, swish. Ingram's triples capped a 13-2 Illinois run and gave the Illini a 61-58 lead. The final frames were highlight-reel stuff: Head drove to set up Augustine for a vicious dunk as the Illini suffocated Wisconsin defensively. When the horn sounded, Ingram lifted his arms into the sky and motioned for the crowd to get up, but there was a deafening silence in the Kohl Center. The streak was dead, and Illinois had come roaring back to life.

Later, standing on the court in silence, Roger Powell Jr. looked past the empty seats and toward the heavens. He had been asked an obvious question: Whether in the wake of a game like this, populated by heroes like that, it wasn't starting to seem as if the Illini were a team of destiny.

"I truly believe," he said, smiling, "that this team is blessed."

The Century Kids

Though Illinois had been ranked No. 1 for weeks, the Wisconsin win still had a feeling of validation about it, and the fervor around Illini basketball reached a whole new peak. Those hot-selling No. 1 T-shirts became even more common, and it was all but impossible to watch local TV or radio without the subject of Illinois basketball coming up.

The timing couldn't have been better. Four days after the Wisconsin game, Illinois hosted its centennial celebration, a party commemorating 100 years of Illini hoops. And for the current players, the feeling was roughly akin to showing up at your high school reunion with a supermodel on your arm.

"It's great to have them coming back when we're having the year we're having," Powell said. "Hopefully everybody's proud."

There was little doubt about that. Lou Henson, recently retired from his head coaching position at New Mexico State, made a last-minute decision to attend the festivities. At a pregame press conference, he lauded the current Illini for their unselfish team play. When Henson waved to the crowd at halftime of Illinois' 89-66 win against Minnesota, he received a thunderous ovation.

But the talk of the weekend was the current crop of players, of their chance to go undefeated and take Illinois to its first-ever national championship. There were countless comparisons to the

Luther Head poses for a photo with Flying Illini legend Steve Bardo, as the two pretend to arm wrestle. The 2005 Illini drew continual comparisons to the 1989 Illini throughout the season. *Robert K. O'Daniell/The News-Gazette*

1989 Flyin' Illini—Illinois' last Final Four team—fueled by a *News-Gazette* special section featuring Luther Head and '89 point guard Steve Bardo posed on the cover as if arm wrestling.

The Illini were thrilled to meet their successors and pay tribute to the players who'd paved the way, even if they weren't exactly well-versed in Illinois hoops history. Deron Williams, talking about the late Dwight "Dike" Eddleman, perhaps the most decorated athlete in Illinois history, called him "Dick" Eddleman. And like most of Weber's players, Brown admitted he'd grown up rooting more for the red and black of Michael Jordan's Chicago Bulls than for the orange and blue.

"I could sit here and lie and tell you I remember, but I don't," Brown said. "I watched a couple games when Kiwane Garris was here because he was from the West Side (of Chicago) and I was staying out there at the time. He was the first guy I knew out of Chicago to go down to Illinois and do his thing."

The old-timers knew all about Brown, though, and they admitted to being more thrilled with Illinois basketball than they'd been in ages. When the weekend ended with its most powerful moment—a photo featuring hundreds of Illinois players, coaches, and support staff, past and present—there was a feeling that the best still lay ahead for the Illini. "You just feel this is a team of destiny and is going to win the championship and be undefeated," former Illinois star Jim Dawson said. But there were plenty of obstacles on the road ahead. The first—and at the time most threatening—would come just two days later, at the Breslin Center in East Lansing, Michigan.

7

ROCK STARS

About 140 miles separate Champaign from Chicago, but it might as well be a million. The University of Illinois welcomes thousands of the Windy City's best and brightest students every year, and the two cities are in the same state, but they operate in different worlds.

"Up in Chicago, you'd have to be a big sports fan to know who I am," Dee Brown said. "In Champaign, I can't go anywhere and not have everybody know me."

In the 2004-05 season, there were times when even that distinction was made more difficult, when the state's biggest city treated the team from small-town Champaign like its own. Still, Chicago was nothing like Champaign. During a season in which the nation fell in love with Illinois, the passion for the Illini always was strongest at home. And in Champaign-Urbana, the love for Illinois basketball was as strong as it's ever been.

The Illini found that out early. A day after the Illini romped Wake Forest, Roger Powell Jr. walked across campus to find a parking attendant standing dangerously close to his charcoal-gray Chrysler LHS. Powell approached with caution. But he needn't have worried. One look at Powell was all it took for a forgiving parking attendant.

"He let me put change in the meter," Powell said. "I think he was going to give me a ticket."

That was but a taste of things to come, a precursor to the city, state and nation's season-long love affair with all things Illinois basketball. In the months after, Powell and his teammates would be treated like kings. Or, perhaps more accurately, like rock stars.

Wherever the Illini went, fans were sure to follow. And though any successful Illinois basketball team is bound to build an intense fan following, none was ever treated to quite the level of adulation that would become a part of day-to-day life for the Illini.

"I thought about it when we played Oregon up in Chicago," Deron Williams said. "I just thought, 'Man, all these people know who we are.' It's a weird feeling, because we're just a bunch of college kids. I guess some people think we're special, like we're some kind of extraterrestrials or something, but we're just college kids who happen to play basketball."

Sign of the Times

Kids have always wanted Illinois players' autographs. A few Illini fans are usually scrambling after games to get a basketball signed or to pose for a photo. But in 2004-05, the fever reached a whole new level that the Illini couldn't possibly have been ready for.

"I never thought I'd reach the point where writing my name on a piece of paper would make somebody happy," Dee Brown said. "It's funny to me. But if it makes a kid or somebody feel good, I'll do it. It's, like, four seconds of my life. It's a big 'D,' a big 'B,' and then you move on. I don't have any problem with it."

It's a good thing, because Brown signed nonstop during his junior year. And he wasn't alone. Each Illini player was approached every day, usually more than once. Even on campus, sometimes a safe haven from autograph seekers, Illinois players couldn't escape their adoring public. Not that they always wanted to. Classmates sought autographs. Students would stop players on the Quad and ask to take a photo. The Illini might have had their images captured by more cell phone cameras than any team in college hoops history.

"People would always ask, 'Do you get tired of it?'" Luther Head said. "You can't get tired of something you do every day. Eventually you just have to get used to it. It feels good. You don't

James Augustine signs autographs for fans during the centennial celebration. It's a wonder that the team had any strength left in their wrists to shoot the ball after all the autographs they signed throughout the year.
Heather Coit/The News-Gazette

want to sign all the time, but you like the support, so you do it. I liked when people were coming up to us saying supportive things. If they wanted me to sign a shirt or whatever, I'd do it."

In fact, Head came to get such a high off the feeling that he wanted to share it. By his senior year, Head had been through more than his bit of ups and downs. And the outpouring of love that fans showed him touched him deeply in his final season in orange and blue. He wanted to spread the love.

"Sometimes, I would go up to people and ask for their autograph," Head said. "Just random people on campus. I really did that. I just wanted them to have that feeling of somebody asking for an autograph."

So Many Basketballs,
So Little Time

From the opening day of practice to the weeks after the Final Four, the Illini always were in demand from autograph seekers. But the peak of their popularity came—as it typically does—around the holidays. The week before final exams, Illinois had so many autograph requests that the team's meeting room at the Ubben Basketball Complex was literally overrun with basketballs and posters to sign.

"There was no table space," administrative assistant Rod Cardinal said. "We just lined all the tables with basketballs, and we gave each guy a marker and he would go right down the line, signing one basketball right after the other."

And that was just the basketballs. There also were posters and pictures and T-shirts and even Illinois flags to sign. The players did so diligently. But it was tiresome work.

"I bet I signed 1,000 things," Brown said of the week before finals, and that might have been a conservative estimate. In addition to the hundreds of requests waiting each day at Ubben, players often signed on campus or at the mall during their holiday shopping.

"Somebody asked me to sign some underwear once," Brown said. "I don't mind it. Just as long as I'm not out getting something to eat or I'm not out hanging out with my friends or whatever, I'll sign."

Even Brown tired, though, of the holiday rush. In fact, all his teammates burned out on signing items they knew would end up under Christmas trees. Before practice, after practice and in their own spare time, the Illini were perfecting their signatures, and it got a little old. With one exception: Weber and his staff heard not one complaint when items came from troops stationed in Iraq. When one troop requested an Illini flag to fly from their station in Iraq, the Illinois players lined up to sign it, all without hesitation.

"They're doing a great job over there, and we're thinking about them, so any chance we get to do something for them, we jump at it," Head said.

But not every autograph seeker had such pure motives. Several times during the early season, Illinois athletic department officials sent cease-and-desist letters to eBay auctioneers who put auto-graphed Illinois items up for sale on the online auction site.

"It got so crazy," Illinois sports information director Kent Brown said, "that there were people selling Fred Nkemdi stuff on there."

Webermania!

Ten days before Christmas, Weber got his surest sign yet of the passion fans felt for his program. It came two weeks after the Illini had pounded No. 1-ranked Wake Forest and a week after Illinois had reached the No. 1 ranking itself. That night, Weber arrived at Gameday Spirit, a sports apparel store in the Campustown district of Champaign, expecting a nice turnout for his scheduled autograph signing to benefit charity. His team, after all, was 9-0 and coming off a blowout win against previously unbeaten Oregon. Optimism was soaring, and with only Cincinnati appearing to be a serious threat, the Illini seemed a near-lock to finish the non-conference season with a perfect record.

So Weber knew he'd draw a crowd. He had no idea just how big, though. Hundreds of fans showed up at the store, many hoping to get the coach's autograph on a Christmas present for a loved one.

Players weren't the only ones hounded for autographs. Coach Bruce Weber signed his name a fair share of times as well. Here he signs copies of *A Century of Orange and Blue* during the centennial celebration.
Heather Coit/The News-Gazette

They lined up out the door and down the block, so many clamoring to get in for the signing that Weber couldn't possibly have accommodated them all in the hour he'd allotted.

"It was pandemonium," said Gameday Spirit manger Cory Shumard. "We had never had anything like it."

Eventually, Shumard had to close and lock the doors to the store, and the many fans who didn't make it in were out of luck. Though Weber had hoped to sign for all of them, time caught up to him. His hand was cramping by the time he finished, and even then, he hadn't satisfied the masses.

"There were people outside literally banging on the door," Weber said. "I never expected that. That was one of those situations where it really hits you that people are responding."

Drawing the Line

Four days after the near-mob scene at the store, it hit Weber just how taxing fan demand had become on his players. On the court, Illinois' 93-56 rout of Valparaiso on December 19 was mostly uneventful. All five Illini starters scored in double figures, Brown made four three-pointers, and Weber's team cruised to a 26-point halftime lead in a game that was never in doubt. Afterward, though, the fan crush hit home for Weber.

The coach had invited friends from out of town to the game, and hoped that the game's afternoon start would afford him the rare opportunity to enjoy dinner at home with the visitors. Weber's postgame activities—a radio show, a press conference, and an a post-press conference meeting with beat writers—often take as long as an hour and a half. On this day, after a long discussion with the media—less about the game itself than about the state of his team—Weber finally got in his SUV for the drive home. He called his friend to let him know that he was on the way.

"He answers his cell, and he's like, 'We're still at the Assembly Hall,'" Weber said. "And I'm thinking, 'How in the world did I beat him out of there?' Turns out, his son wanted Dee's autograph, and they were still in line. I had done all my postgame stuff, and Dee and Deron were still there signing."

It hit Weber then. "We had to make some changes," he said. For the rest of the season, players' parents were allowed in the meeting rooms in the Assembly Hall's tunnels, allowing players to meet with their parents after the game without strolling back out onto the court, where they could be spied by autograph seekers. That gave players the option of slipping out the door after games without drawing a crowd, though most of them still wandered onto the court after they had showered and changed, looking to meet up with friends. Even when they didn't, Weber said, they couldn't go uninterrupted on their way home.

"They'd come outside, and there would be people waiting on the way to their cars," Weber said. "It was amazing."

Hit the Road

As wild as things got in Champaign, Weber was almost grateful for the chance to take his team out of town. He'd leave as early as he could for most trips in the hopes of getting his players away from the circus atmosphere that had permeated the Illinois campus. Little did he know how far it would follow him. Everywhere Illinois went during the season, its fans followed. And though Weber was grateful for—and sometimes amazed by—the support, it created its own share of problems.

There came a point in the season when the Illini couldn't so much as get off the bus without drawing a crowd, and Weber and his support staff had to invent creative ways of avoiding the throngs of fans at every stop along the road. When the Illini went to Chicago in December to play Oregon, they entered the downtown Hilton through a side door, then took a back way to the elevators in an effort to get to their rooms without fanfare. By the end of the season, Weber and his players were entering every hotel through the kitchen and taking freight elevators to their floors.

"It was crazy, man," Head said. "You ain't never seen love like that. We had to go sneaking around."

By NCAA tournament time, well-wishers and autograph seekers had become so commonplace—with Illinois fans overtaking each tournament site the Illini visited—that Weber had security guards assigned to Illinois' hotel floors. Nobody got on or off the floor without their permission. The move was designed to keep Weber's players from being distracted. But it had other benefits as well.

"It really freed me up," Weber said. "I didn't have to do bed check. I didn't have to worry about whether guys were breaking curfew. We had our own security staff to worry about that. And those guys were great. We'd get food delivered and go take some to our security guys. They were like part of the team."

Hotels weren't the only spots where Weber's players were recognized. Sometimes even the coach and players were amazed by the public's reaction to a college basketball team, and never more so than during a trip to Northwestern in January. As is Weber's practice, the Illini arrived in Evanston, Illinois, a day before the game and checked into a local hotel. With a Saturday afternoon start on tap, Weber didn't want his players up late. He also didn't want them cooped up in a hotel on a Friday night. So as a group the Illini went to the movies.

"We went and saw *Coach Carter*," Head said. "It was a real good movie. I think everybody liked it. But it got crazy."

The night was normal enough until the final credits rolled on the movie. That's when the ovation came. It wasn't for Samuel Jackson's performance.

"People were standing up, applauding our players," Weber said.

"This is in Chicago," Williams said. "It wasn't like we were in Champaign. We're in the middle of Chicago at a movie theater, and all these people start clapping—for us. You just have to be like, 'Wow.'"

Showing Their Devotion

Fans didn't have to ask for autographs to show how passionate they were about the Illini. They bought tickets in record numbers and at dizzying speeds, selling out the season long before the first game tipped off. When Illinois hosted its annual "Paint the Hall Orange" night against Wake Forest, it seemed almost anticlimactic. By then, it had become standard practice to show up at the Assembly Hall dressed in orange, and at least three-quarters of the crowd typically displayed the color in some form or another.

"We got this idea that we didn't need to have a special night," Williams said. "We wanted them to show up in orange every night. When they started doing that, it was great. It got us even more pumped up. It made the Hall even tougher to play in."

Fans took the idea to extremes. They wore orange sweaters, orange coats. They wore orange hats. Orange wigs. Even orange aprons—donated to Illinois' Orange Krush student section by the Weber grill company.

"I could put out an orange piece of lettuce and somebody'd pay 10 bucks for it," said Miranda Carr, a manager at the Illini Shop in Champaign's Marketplace Mall.

But wearing orange wasn't enough for some fans, who took their love of the Illini to extremes—none more so than Ceasar Perez. The Illinois student began arriving at games wearing a pair of oversized "Hulk-hand" gloves that he'd painted blue and christened with the orange Illinois logo. To top it off, he covered his bare-chested body in orange paint. He seemed to make an appearance at every Illinois game, garnering something of a cult following. He graced countless newspaper pages, appeared in *Sports Illustrated*, made the back cover of *The News-Gazette's* season in review book, and even started his own webpage, www.mrbluehands.com.

And if that weren't enough, two different rappers wrote and recorded songs about the Illini. One of them, which called out each player by name ("Dee Brown, he be doin' it... Luther Head, he be doin' it...") was sent via e-mail to what seemed like half the Illinois campus and was played on WPGU 107.1-FM, the student-run radio station.

"When I heard it, I was like, 'Are you serious?'" forward James Augustine said. "That's something you just don't ever expect. It was kind of weird, to be honest with you."

It was a little weird for Weber, too. Word of mouth about the songs reached him long before he ever heard either, but Weber—who's more into open J's than Jay-Z—found the musical tribute amusing for its sheer lunacy.

"It's like being the '85 Bears," he said. "Except they don't have us in the video."

They've Got a Krush on You

As usual, though, Illinois' most devoted fans came from its student body, specifically the Orange Krush student support group. Perhaps the most unique such group in the nation, the Krush had evolved from merely a rowdy pack of students at the Assembly Hall to a fully functioning charitable foundation, donating more than a half-million dollars to campus and local programs over a six-year period. Its donations grew exponentially in 2004-05. As had become tradition, members made donations based on the number of three-pointers the Illini made in the season. A school-record 344

The best fans in the country—the Orange Krush student cheering section—root Illinois on during a game against Minnesota. The Krush spent the 2004-05 season raising quite a bit of money—and some hell, too—in support of the Illini. *John Dixon/The News-Gazette*

threes meant record-setting totals in money raised for scholarships and charitable donations.

But for all the good they'd done over the years, the Krush liked to raise a little hell, too, and 2004-05 provided ample opportunity. Orange-clad students taunted visiting coaches and players, and as it had the year before, the Krush mobilized in massive numbers to take its act on the road. When Michigan refused to sell the Krush group tickets to the Wolverines' game against the Illini in Crisler Arena, a member called back, posing as a representative of Chicago-based "Youth Action," a group ostensibly planning to bring a large number of prospective students to Ann Arbor for a campus visit.

Instead, Krush members arrived in town wearing black "Youth Action" T-shirts. They were offered a campus tour and a photo with Wolverines coach Tommy Amaker, then escorted to the game, where they sat together and, during pregame warmups, cheered for Michigan. They even sang "Hail To The Victors" and taunted Illinois players with a chant of "over-rated" as the Illini took the court. Then the public address announcer began the introduction of the starting lineups, and the ruse was complete. Krush members ripped off the black T-shirts to reveal orange ones underneath, and began cheering wildly for the Illini. The stunt, perfectly timed and executed, earned Krush members airtime on ESPN and was the envy of student cheering sections everywhere.

But things didn't always go so smoothly for the Krush. Less well-documented was the group's trip to Iowa City for a rivalry game against Iowa. Despite leaving before dawn on a Saturday, the Krush missed the first five minutes of the game after buses carrying 110 Krush members got lost on the way to Carver-Hawkeye Arena. Still, the Krush found a way to make the most of a bad situation. They sang "Oskee Wow Wow" as they drove through town, many drinking what junior Travis Drury called "homemade juices" on the bus. And when the Krush made its way into Carver-Hawkeye, Illinois fans—there were more than 3,000 of them in the crowd—started to buzz. After the Illini held off Iowa in winning a second hotly contested game of the season against their rivals, players waved to the Illinois fans, and later told reporters that the support had played a role in the win.

"I don't know what these Big Ten teams are thinking letting Illinois fans in the arena," Dee Brown said. "You'll never see that out at our house. Never."

It became a common sight at Big Ten houses, though: orange-clad fans, led by the Krush, coming in droves and often drowning out the home crowd as the Illini pulled away to win. In Iowa City, as the Krush formed a conga line leaving the arena, Illinois fans lined up to give high-fives and celebrate the win. Iowa fans glared as they walked to their cars and drove away. And some did more than glare.

"Some gave us the finger," Drury said. "Including an old lady."

Meet the Press

Weber worried that fans would prove distracting to his players, but they weren't the only outsiders who had Weber concerned. As his team continued to pile up wins, the national media became more and more interested in Illinois. That meant demands on the players' time unlike any in the history of the program.

A writer from the *New York Daily News* spent a few days in town. *Sports Illustrated* went to Brown and Head's off-campus apartment for a story and later a photo shoot with Brown and Williams. *Nike Training Camp*, a documentary series offering inside looks at athletic teams, visited for a week over the holiday break and took its cameras everywhere from the locker room to the sideline, with microphones turned on all the while.

"That got to be a little much," Weber said. "I'd be yelling at somebody on the practice court, I'd turn around, and—boom!— there's a mic or a camera right in my face."

The players didn't mind the training camp video. But as the season wore on, the Illini began to wear down from the constant barrage of media requests. Though as few as two or three reporters consistently showed up to cover practices, Brown, Head, Williams, Augustine, and Roger Powell Jr. routinely had telephone interviews to conduct afterward. The most popular Illini sometimes found themselves in a rush to get to Illinois athletes' nightly training table for dinner before it closed.

"I love talking to you," Brown told me one day before the NCAA tournament. "You've been here. All these other people, it's like they jumped on the bandwagon or something. You get tired of doing the same thing, answering the same questions all the time."

The media burnout resulted in a pair of surprising decisions in January. First, the Illini voted—almost unanimously—not to allow ESPN to follow the team for episodes of its behind-the-scenes documentary series, *The Season*. After the *Nike Training Camp* experience, the Illini were ready to scale back their television appearances.

"We just wanted to just be ourselves and not have to worry about the cameras," Head said. "Plus, we had a good thing going. We didn't want to mess with it."

Weber allowed his players to vote, but he made no secret of the fact that he hoped to keep ESPN out of his practices. He'd been through a similar documentary process before, when, as the coach at Southern Illinois, he'd granted MTV an all-access look at his team. But with so much on the line in 2004-05—and with his team's chemistry so perfect—Weber didn't want to repeat the process. He worried that the show would paint a few players as stars, and that those who didn't get as much airtime might resent it.

Eventually, he came to worry that his players would resent the media in general. That's part of the reason that, for the first time during his short stay in Champaign, he instituted a media blackout in the heart of the Big Ten season. In late January, as Illinois prepared to travel to Wisconsin for a game against the Badgers, Weber shut off reporters' access to his players for five days. It's a fairly common practice in most programs, but at Illinois, where media accessibility has become a trademark and where players typically are available for comment daily during the season, it was a startling move.

"I could sense they were getting tired, and I didn't know if it was a physical fatigue or a mental fatigue," Weber said. "The physical fatigue, I could control. I cut down practices. We'd go hard for shorter periods. But the mental fatigue, there was only so much I could do. I couldn't get them out of classes. So talking to [the media] was all I could think of."

His players appreciated the break. And coincidentally or not, they responded, rallying from eight points down in the second half to beat Wisconsin and snap the Badgers' 38-game homecourt winning streak. After the Illini had celebrated a stirring win, Brown and Williams marched into the press room almost anxious to discuss the game with a horde of reporters.

"It's been a while," Williams said.

8

RUNNING AWAY WITH THE BIG TEN

There's an old saying that goes, "unless you're the lead dog, the scenery never changes." Illinois had spent three months out in front of the college basketball pack, and yet to the Fighting Illini, the scenery always seemed pretty much the same. Each week brought a new challenge, and a new round of doubters.

By the end of the first month of the Big Ten schedule, Illinois had dispatched Wisconsin at the Kohl Center and had won its seven conference games by an average of almost 15 points. The Illini hadn't been beaten, and they'd only been seriously challenged in two of those games. But in newspapers, across the Internet and—most notably—on television, Illinois still had its doubters, pundits proclaiming North Carolina as the nation's best team. It was hardly an outlandish statement. The Tar Heels hadn't remained unscathed as Illinois had, but Roy Williams was blessed with far and away the nation's most talented team. And Carolina, a college basketball blueblood, played in the Atlantic Coast Conference, widely—and annually—regarded as the nation's best basketball league.

As ESPN analysts like Dick Vitale and Digger Phelps continued to assert that the Tar Heels, not the Illini, were the nation's best team, Illinois players began to fume. They bristled at questions about the subject and despite being ranked the unanimous No. 1 team in both major college basketball polls, they often turned discussions with reporters into diatribes on respect. Or lack thereof.

"There was this feeling like, 'What else do we have to do?'" Deron Williams said. "We got tired of it."

Illinois' defiance reached its apex in late January, as the Illini prepared for a February 1 game against Michigan State in East Lansing, Michigan. With only two days between the centennial celebration game and the meeting with the Spartans, Illinois' trip north didn't have the Super Bowl-like hype that surrounded, say, the Missouri game, which often had a finals week's worth of buildup. But for two days, the Illini and Spartans took up most of the ink and airtime devoted to college basketball. And the general consensus seemed to be this: That Illinois was the better team, but that Michigan State would pull the upset.

Tom Izzo's Spartans became a hip pick to hand the Illini their first loss. It happened on ESPN, on Internet message boards, even in *The News-Gazette*, where I picked against Illinois for the first time all season. The Illini checked into their hotel in East Lansing on January 30, and when Williams turned on ESPN, he saw experts on two popular shows—*Around the Horn* and *Pardon the Interruption*—picking Michigan State to win the game. Particularly infuriating to the Illini was that regular *Around the Horn* guest Jay Mariotti, a columnist at the *Chicago Sun-Times*, expected the Spartans to win. As the highest-profile media personality from the state of Illinois, Mariotti's prediction carried extra sting.

"I mean, he's a Chicago guy," Dee Brown said.

Pedal to the Mettle

Michigan State was the only team in the Big Ten that pushed the ball up the court as aggressively as did Illinois. Playing in the Breslin Center—where the Spartans had won 95 of their previous 101 games—only amped up Michigan State's pace. "We only know how to play one way," Izzo said the day before the game, bristling at the suggestion that the Spartans would slow down their breakneck pace for fear of allowing Illinois to get out and run. Izzo would come to regret it. And the rest of the Big Ten took note.

In perhaps its most flawless performance of the season, Illinois pushed the pace and pummeled Michigan State in front of its home crowd, rolling to an 81-68 win that seemed to finally put doubts to rest. Illinois shot 57 percent from the floor and answered every Michigan State challenge. When the Spartans put together an early second-half run to close within three points, the Illini scored 10 straight points—eight by Luther Head, on a dunk and two three-pointers—to quiet the rowdy Spartan crowd and the "Izzone" student section. In one second-half stretch, the Illini made 12 consecutive shots against a team known as much for its hard-nosed defense as for its transition offense.

"It was just one of those nights," Roger Powell Jr. said. "One of those nights where everything worked."

Indeed it was. Illinois made 13 three-pointers. It hung tough on the boards. And it committed just 10 turnovers. Michigan State's only late, second-half push was Illini-aided. The Spartans closed to within seven, thanks in part to a technical foul on Brown. After he took an inbound pass late in the game, Brown was fouled, and he took exception to what he thought was a hard foul by Michigan State guard Tim Bograkos. Brown's temper got the best of him. Before he strolled to the free throw line, he put an elbow in Bograkos' midsection. Brown didn't hit Bograkos with much force, and he'd tried to do it discreetly. But a referee caught the move, and hit Brown with a technical.

As the Spartans went to the free throw line—they made all 13 of their attempts in the game—Brown gathered his teammates and did what he'd already done twice to Bograkos. He apologized.

"I told everybody I shouldn't have done it, and that I was going to get it back," Brown said. "That's what I said: 'I'm going to get it back.'"

A few possessions later, Head rebounded a Spartan miss and tossed an outlet to Brown. The so-called "One-Man Fast Break" streaked downcourt, and as he went to the basket drew a foul from Michigan State's Chris Hill. Brown's lay-up attempt kissed its way in for a three-point play try.

"I told you!" Brown screamed as his teammates pulled him to his feet for hugs and high-fives. "I told you!" Brown's ensuing free throw extended the Illini lead back to 10 points, and the final minutes were a foregone conclusion. When the final horn sounded,

Deron Williams and the Illini were ready for Michigan State in their only meeting of 2005 at the Breslin Center in East Lansing, Michigan. The Illinois backcourt accounted for 54 points and 11 three-pointers in the Illini's impressive 81-68 win. *AP/WWP*

Weber and Izzo, longtime friends dating to their days as assistants in the Big Ten, shook hands at halfcourt. "You've got a real chance to win it all," Izzo told Weber.

The celebration on the Illini sideline was subdued compared to the one at Wisconsin. Illinois had expected to beat the Spartans, and the players behaved as such. They congratulated one another, shook hands with their Michigan State counterparts and walked off the court with their arms raised toward the few Illinois fans who had been able to score a ticket.

"I can see how you would've thought they'd beat us, on paper," Williams said afterward in the tunnel leading to Illinois' bus. "But we never thought that way. Never."

Illinois had stomped on Michigan State's heart, and left its doubters with little ammunition.

"Keep picking against us," Brown said. "See what happens."

Dee Brown to the Rescue

Illinois had its hangover game five days later, beating Indiana 60-47 on a sluggish Super Bowl Sunday. The Illini jumped out to a 20-3 lead but led just 26-20 at halftime. Against Indiana's sloweddown offense, Illinois never was able to mount a game-ending run despite four players scoring in double figures and 11 assists from Williams. Illinois led by double figures for the final 15:33 of the game but couldn't turn the game into a blowout.

Somewhere, Tommy Amaker was watching. The Michigan coach, trying to rebuild a once-proud program ravaged by NCAA probation and player defections, had built a team of quick-footed athletes and streaky outside shooters, devoid of true point guard play. But he also had a collection of bruisers in the post. And in watching Indiana, Amaker realized his only prayer against Illinois was to play the game at a snail's pace and hope to frustrate the Illini.

"In two days, they completely changed their style of play," Weber said. "You really have to give [Amaker] a ton of credit for that."

It probably didn't help that the Illini had their gameday routine changed when fog struck Champaign late on a Monday night, when

Dee Brown ignited the Illini in their 57-51 road win against Michigan. Brown came up with several critical steals down the stretch, and chipped in a team-best 16 points. *AP/WWP*

Illinois was scheduled to fly to Ann Arbor, Michigan, for a Tuesday game. The team spent hours at the university's Willard Airport before being told that their flight would not depart. They went home and flew to Ann Arbor at 8 a.m. the day of the game.

"It probably didn't have a big impact," Weber said. "But they didn't get their nap, the power nap they like to get."

That nap would come during the game, unfortunately, when the Wolverines lulled Illinois to sleep. Amaker's decision to milk the clock worked like clockwork in the first half. The Illini shot 37 percent and trailed 28-24 at halftime to a Michigan team that had lost six straight entering the Illinois game.

"We were mad at halftime," James Augustine said. "Guys were just mad."

But Illinois struggled to take its anger out on Michigan. Early in the second half, the Wolverines built an eight-point lead as Illinois went through its worst offensive drought of the season. In a stretch that bridged the end of the first half and the start of the second, the Illini went 12 minutes without a basket. To turn the tide, Illinois looked to its defense. Michigan had just eight field goals in the second half, and after the Illini whittled the lead to 39-35, Brown came alive—and in the process probably clinched the Big Ten's Player of the Year award. Brown had three steals in the span of just over a minute, turning them into seven points—including a three-point play that gave Illinois the lead for good.

"That's the player we've seen over the years in this league," Amaker said. "Electrifying."

But Brown saved his best play for the finish. Late in the game, he drove to the basket and, cut off by two Michigan defenders, spun in midair and delivered a picture-perfect behind-the-back pass to Augustine.

"It's a miracle I didn't throw it right to the bench," Brown said.

Instead it went right to Augustine, who threw down a thunderous two-handed dunk that helped ice the Illini win and was on every highlight reel that night. It was the kind of play Brown was known for attempting, but not always completing. Augustine admitted later that he'd dropped several such passes in practice over the years.

"If I had dropped that," Augustine said. "I would have been in a lot of trouble."

Instead, he finished, and Brown, who finished the game with a team-high 16 points, was a hero. His clutch performance—in one of Illinois' only tight games—came during an ESPN broadcast, and probably gave him an edge over Williams and Head in the conference player of the year race. He also went on to win the league's defensive player of the year award, no doubt buoyed by his four-steal performance in the Illini's 57-51 defeat of Michigan.

"He loves the big moment," Weber said of Brown. "And when it's a close game, he's even better. Where some guys feel the pressure of the big moment, he never seems to."

Motivational Madness

After dispatching Wisconsin at home in an easier-than-expected 70-59 win, Illinois headed to Penn State. It's said that there are two sports seasons in State College, Pennsylvania: the football season and football-recruiting season. But the sleepy little mountain town has been known to come alive for hoops from time to time, given the right motivation. Penn State and its fans had plenty on February 16, when top-ranked Illinois came to town, and the Nittany Lions were looking for one of the biggest upsets in school history.

A local eatery, Wings Over Happy Valley, had upped the ante for Penn State fans, offering 10 free buffalo wings to any fan with a ticket stub if the Nittany Lions could knock off the Illini. "I felt bad for all the chickens," said Weber, whose team could have been responsible for 109,000 free wings had it lost.

Illinois needn't have worried. The Illini led 52-30 by halftime and rolled to an 83-63 win. Afterward, players shouted "No wings! No wings tonight!" as they sprinted back to the locker room. "If we had lost, we might have gone and had some," Head joked. In truth, Illinois really didn't need the extra motivation, but Weber was glad to have it. As the season wore on and the blowout wins mounted, Weber struggled to find buttons that he could push to have his team respond. But it was not for lack of trying.

In the season's opening weekend, he had showed his team high-lights of Michigan State's opening-night win against Florida A&M and challenged his players to play as hard—and win as big—against the Rattlers on a Sunday as the Spartans had on a Friday. Throughout the year, Weber used media disrespect as a reoccurring theme. Every time Digger Phelps or Jay Mariotti doubted his team, Weber drove the point home. When even late in the Big Ten season Illinois was ranked fifth in the Ratings Percentage Index, a formula that helps determine a team's NCAA tournament seeding, Weber pointed to it as proof that the Illini still had a reason to play hard. He used the promise of jewelry, too, as a motivator, telling his players, "Being No. 1 is nice, but it doesn't get you a ring. There are only three ways you can get a ring. You win a league championship, you get to the Final Four or you win a national championship."

As Michigan State came down the stretch, Weber rooted hard for the Spartans—not just because he and Izzo were close friends, but because he wanted to create a sense of urgency for his own players. With only two conference losses, Michigan State was a theoretical threat as long as it kept winning. Weber would tell his team, "They aren't going to lose again," even when he wasn't sure if it was true.

"It was that kind of year; we kept winning games, and I wasn't sure what to say," Weber said. "It got to a point where I was like, 'What can I write on the board today?'"

Cold Chills, Hot Brown

Headed down to the wire, it looked as though Illinois' biggest challenge might come at Iowa. Though the Hawkeyes had lost leading scorer Pierce Pierce since giving the Illini a fight in Champaign, they were hungry for a statement-making home-court win that could boost their NCAA tournament hopes. And even without Pierce, Iowa's long, versatile backcourt found ways to give Illinois fits. Despite a huge turnout of Illinois fans, the Hawkeyes stayed in the game from the opening tip to the final minutes. Maybe they got a lift from a bit of unplanned sabotage.

Dee Brown tugs at his jersey, which became a popular trend among players across the nation during 2004-05. *AP/WWP*

In years past, Illinois had been reluctant to stay downtown in Iowa City, for fear that Iowa students might get overzealous in taunting or playing pranks on their hated rivals from Champaign. But hotels in the outlying areas weren't as spacious—nor as swank— as the downtown Sheraton hotel that rested in the midst of Iowa City's campus bar scene. Reluctantly, Rod Cardinal, the longtime trainer who still booked the Illini's travel plans, gave in and reserved the Illini rooms in the city's nicest hotel.

Bed-check and curfew, strictly enforced as always, kept Illinois out of trouble. But as it turned out, Iowa students weren't the only potential risks. The Illini awoke for a Saturday morning game anxious to warm up and get to Carver-Hawkeye Arena. The warming up would prove difficult. On a bitter, blistery Iowa morning—a considerable snow would blow through hours after the game—Illinois players staggered to their showers for a rude awakening.

"There was no hot water," Augustine said. "None."

Indeed, sometime early in the morning, the entire hotel lost its hot-water supply. Shaving was an adventure. Showers were downright chilling.

"I think they did it on purpose," Brown said.

There was no proof of that—nor any that the cool showers contributed to Illinois' chilly start. The Illini made three of their nine first-half three-pointers and finished with only five threes for the game; meanwhile, Iowa spent the afternoon making charge after charge only to be swatted down. Brown was the chief culprit, tying Williams with a team-high 18 points, including a crucial three-pointer that resulted in his famous jersey tug—a photo op that would grace the cover of the following week's *Sports Illustrated*.

But on a day best remembered for cold showers, it was Nick Smith who rained in the biggest shot, a three-pointer from the corner in the final minute that beat the shot clock and broke Iowa's back. In his postgame press conference, Iowa coach Steve Alford pointed to Smith in illustrating just how difficult it was to beat a team with so many offensive options who remained so cool under pressure. ("I mean, look who's making plays for them," Alford said. "Nick Smith.")

"We're hard to rattle," Head said. "Cold showers, whatever."

A Dish in Time

Returning home to their own warm showers for a February 23 matchup with Northwestern, the Illini outscored the Wildcats 42-3 from three-point range and 84-48 overall. The game was notable for little, outside of Powell's first assist of the Big Ten season. Always an undersized workhorse in the post, Powell had expanded his game as a senior. He had grown comfortable with his jump shot again, stepping behind the three-point line as he had his sophomore year to become a viable threat from long range.

But one facet of the game still eluded Powell: passing. When he joked that he'd made it a goal to get more assists than Brown, Williams, or Head in a game, Brown cracked, "I could shoot 25 threes and still get more assists than you."

"We gave it to him pretty good," Williams said.

But when Powell dished off to Head for a basket, he finally ended that chatter.

"If you saw him running down the court, he was holding up a No. 1," Weber said. "It wasn't for us being No. 1, it was for his first assist. He was pretty happy."

Celebrate Good Times

A season Illinois fans hoped would last forever was nearing its conclusion, and even Weber was amazed by what his team was accomplishing. The Illini could have sluggish practices, then flip the switch at gametime and put on a dominant performance. With 27 straight victories, they had secured their place among the great teams in Big Ten history, even as members of the 1976 Indiana Hoosiers—the last undefeated national champion in NCAA hoops—rooted for them to lose.

Weber wanted his team focused on the future, on the Big Ten and NCAA tournaments, but he knew his team deserved a special celebration on Senior Night, and not just for its departing players. As Illinois prepared to host Purdue in its final home game, Michigan State was coming off a loss to Indiana that had clinched the Big Ten title for the Illini. Weber had been rooting for the Spartans, hoping to keep his team playing with a sense of urgency. Still, he wanted to commemorate the Big Ten title on what would be one of the most emotional nights of the season.

Besides bidding farewell to seniors Head, Powell, Smith, Jack Ingram, and Fred Nkemdi, Illinois was saying goodbye to Gene Keady, the Purdue coach and Weber's longtime mentor, who would make his last visit to the Assembly Hall as an opposing coach. Weber and his staff presented Keady with a string of gifts, including a

Illinois players (left to right) Fred Nkemdi, Roger Powell Jr., Jack Ingram, Nick Smith, and Luther Head are recognized during Senior Night at the Assembly Hall. *John Dixon/The News-Gazette*

Weber grill, a cell phone for keeping in touch during his retirement, a pair of suits from a Chicago tailor, and a lifetime honorary membership in the Orange Krush.

Weber's players presented Keady's team with a walloping. Brown hit eight three-pointers against Purdue, apparently shrugging off *Sports Illustrated's* cover jinx, and Illinois took command early in an 84-50 win. The Illini's seniors—honored in a ceremony before the game—had quiet nights, but Brown and Williams combined for 48 points in what would prove to be Williams' final game at the Assembly Hall.

"I knew. Even then I knew," Williams said after the season and he declared himself eligible for the NBA draft. "I was telling myself, 'This is it.' I wanted to have a big night. Go out on top."

He did. After the final horn sounded, Illinois players celebrated on the court as confetti fell from the Assembly Hall rafters and a video on the arena's video board showed highlights from the season. Several Illinois players passed a microphone to say thanks to the fans who had stayed to celebrate. More than an hour later, in an almost-empty Hall, Brown considered the possibility that he might yet return to the building at the end of the season—to celebrate a national championship.

"It would be lovely," he said. "Can you imagine?"

Pushing for Perfection

Though he'd employed any number of motivational tools during the season, Weber had steered clear of the most popular topic among fans and the media. He didn't want to address the possibility of Illinois going undefeated, either for the regular season or the entire year. But that doesn't mean his players weren't excited by the possibility.

"Thirty-nine and 0," Brown said after the Purdue game. "We got 10 left."

That would mean winning in the regular-season finale at Ohio State, sweeping the Big Ten tournament and winning the six games required to win the NCAA championship. Weber had done the math, too. And though Weber didn't want to discuss it, he couldn't control it being discussed everywhere else. As Illinois prepared for a Sunday game at Ohio State, there were three days of nonstop hype about the possibility of college basketball's first perfect season in 29 years.

St. Joseph's had gone unbeaten through the regular season the year before, but had lost in the Atlantic 10 tournament, then fallen a game short of the Final Four. And the Hawks' coach, Phil Martelli, was a popular man down the stretch of the season, fielding almost as many questions about Illinois as about a controversial game in which one of his players had been injured by a Temple player who was instructed by coach John Chaney to commit hard fouls.

"Every call I get about the Illini is, 'Wouldn't it be better for them to take a loss?'" said Martelli, one of the game's great characters. "I don't understand how you take a loss. So you throw a game? Won't Bruce Weber get arrested for that? I'm not a big fan of throwing a game. Bruce Weber seems like a nice guy, but I don't know how well he'd do in prison."

While Martelli was lighthearted, some fans were not. When *The News-Gazette* ran a headline across the top of our Sunday morning sports page that read "30-0" atop a story about Illinois' quest for regular-season perfection, fans were immediately upset. Rumors— still unconfirmed—had the headline making its way by fax from Central Illinois to the desk of Ohio State coach Thad Matta, in Columbus, Ohio. Matta would have received it in time to motivate his players. Whether it was that headline or simply the opportunity to spoil Illinois' season, something got the Buckeyes ready to play on March 6 when the Illini came to town.

The Shot Heard 'Round Ohio

Ohio State was eligible to play in the Big Ten tournament, but with a relatively shorthanded roster, Matta had little chance of winning that. And despite entering the Illinois game with 18 wins, the Buckeyes had no shot at the NCAA tournament thanks to self-imposed sanctions in the wake of recruiting violations. A win against Illinois, therefore, would make Ohio State's season.

But early on, at least, it was the Illini who played like the team in a make-or-break game. Despite shooting just 42 percent in the first half, Illinois built an 11-point halftime lead, and looked to be on the way to completing perfection. But just as they had at home the year before, the Buckeyes rallied in the second half. Spurred on by a Schottenstein Center crowed working hard to drown out the Illini faithful, Ohio State climbed back into the game with its defense.

Illinois led 64-58 with 3:23 to play, but costly turnovers and missed shots down the stretch kept the Illini from scoring again. And coming out of a timeout in the closing seconds, Ohio State went for the jugular. Forward Matt Sylvester already had scored 22 points, five more than his previous career high. He'd made a three-pointer. He'd posted up. He'd driven to the basket and drawn fouls. Conventional wisdom had Ohio State going inside, though, to center Terence Dials, who had scored 21 points. A few possessions earlier, Sylvester had airballed a three-point attempt. Dials had been unstoppable, though. And the basketball adage says to go for the tie at home and to shoot for the win on the road.

Matta didn't go conventional. Instead, Sylvester launched a three-pointer that swished with 5.1 seconds to play, and when the Buckeyes spoiled Illinois' quick-hit play downcourt and then a Roger Powell Jr. three-pointer at the buzzer missed, the dream died. Ohio State fans stormed the court, taunting disgusted Illinois players who appeared numb as they pushed through the masses to get to the locker room.

"Walking off the court, I was really focused on, 'Where do we go from here? How do we get better?'" Powell said. "That's the way you've got to be. You can't live for yesterday. You've got to live for tomorrow."

Brown, who had shot three for 11, looked most distraught of all. A blank expression on his face, he walked to the locker room, then emerged trying to avoid the media, answering each question he was asked with, "They played good basketball." Days later, Weber would quip that Matta was "a genius" for his strategy. "Go to the guy who just airballed," Weber said. "Brilliant."

It was clear that the loss stung. But the Illini said later it also got their attention. It forced them to focus on the task at hand. The postseason was about to begin, and the Illini had been waiting a long time for their moment.

"If we had gone into March undefeated and lost in the first round of the NCAA tournament, nobody would think twice about our season," Augustine said. "It's how you finish that counts."

9

TRAGEDY AND TRIUMPH

As winter shifted to spring—by college basketball's standards, if not by Mother Nature's—so, too, did the Illini's focus shift. With the first loss out of the way and a Big Ten championship in tow, it was time to focus on winning two tournaments: the Big Ten and the NCAA. In preparation, practices, always contentious, moved to a new level of competitiveness. To the outsider, an Illinois practice might have appeared an exercise in bad chemistry, an example of 14 people who truly did not like each other.

"People would probably think we hate each other," Deron Williams said. "We got pretty heated [in practice]."

The mercury rose to new levels in the days leading up to the postseason. After a possession in which six-foot-10 James Augustine missed three short shots, Williams took the ball from him, took two steps and rose to throw down a one-handed dunk.

"I'm 6-3," Williams barked. "How hard is that shit? Dunk the ball!"

It was part of the 2004-05 Fighting Illni's unique personality that a display like that never had a lingering effect—other than to get the target's attention. Often Augustine or Roger Powell Jr. would take verbal abuse from the guards in practice, only to respond with stronger play.

"You have to be able to take that and not take it personally," Dee Brown said. "It comes with being competitive....That's Illinois basketball."

That heated competitiveness was more apparent than ever as the Big Ten tournament loomed. Still stung by the loss at Ohio State, the Illini were more focused than ever to validate their season. Doubters had emerged again. Though Illinois had remained the nation's No. 1 team in both The Associated Press and ESPN/*USA Today* coaches' polls, North Carolina had again become the popular pick to win the national championship. There were doubts about Illinois' post presence, questions as to how the Illini would respond to the adversity of a close game, which it had seen so few times over the course of the Big Ten season. As Bruce Weber's team prepared for the Big Ten tournament, though, no one in the Illinois basketball camp knew just how much the team—or its coach—was about to have its resiliency tested.

A Shock to the System

It was rare for Dawn Weber to see her sons coach in person. Bruce Weber's widowed mother loved basketball, loved to follow his teams at Purdue and Southern Illinois and Illinois, and loved to keep close tabs on David Weber's team at Glenbrook North High School in the Chicago suburbs. One of Bruce Weber's gifts to his mother had been a satellite dish that allowed her to watch all of Illinois' games from her home outside Milwaukee.

But with the Big Ten tournament taking place in Chicago, a shorter drive from home, and with Bruce's team having enjoyed such success in 2004-05, there was no keeping Dawn Weber away. The Weber family would have a reunion of sorts in Chicago. David's Glenbrook North team was in the Illinois state playoffs, but he would make it to as many games as he could. Dawn intended to see them all.

But when she arrived at the United Center on a blustery Friday morning, something wasn't right. As she waited to enter the arena for Illinois' game against Northwestern, she felt tightness and pain in her chest. She told her family of the problem—insisting that Bruce Weber was not to be told until after the game—and was taken to Rush University Medical Center an hour before Illinois was to tip off against Northwestern.

The game itself was hardly memorable to begin with, and given how the day would progress, it's become a complete afterthought, more so than any of the 39 games Illinois played in 2004-05. The Illini didn't get off to the blazing start many fans expected them to in light of the Ohio State loss. They were in an early funk, in fact, and Northwestern led early in the first half. Still, despite nine first-half turnovers, Illinois led by 16 at halftime and went on to a 68-51 win behind Augustine's 15 points and eight rebounds.

The questions in Weber's postgame press conference centered mostly on the turnovers (Illinois finished with 16), and on the game ahead. There were some doubts about the Illini's depth. Weber wanted to see how his bench would hold up if the Illini were fortunate enough to play three games in three days. Weber walked off the podium after that press conference ready for his standard postgame procedure. He'd stand in the hall outside the Illinois locker room and answer more questions for reporters, then—perhaps an hour or more after the final horn sounded—he'd meet his family courtside. But he knew almost immediately that his routine would change. Megan Weber pulled her husband aside as he stepped down from the dais. "It's your mom," she told him.

Word Spreads Quickly

Coach Weber left immediately for Rush University Medical Center, where he would spend virtually all of that Friday night. Back at the United Center, word circulated quickly. Illinois sports information director Kent Brown informed beat writers and television reporters that Dawn Weber had been hospitalized, and soon, even Illinois fans in the stands were aware of her condition. She would undergo heart surgery.

Meanwhile, the tournament carried on. Illinois' assistant coaches knew that Weber would spend the day at the hospital, but they stayed behind to scout. Wayne McClain watched the Minnesota/Indiana game—the winner would face the Illini—and then left to work on the scouting report for the next day. Jay Price and Tracy Webster stayed to scout the evening session.

In the press room, it was one of the strangest days in the history of the Illinois beat. There had been a game played. The Illini had advanced to the second round of the tournament, and certainly that merited mention. But there was a scramble, too, to learn about Dawn Weber's condition. The press room at the United Center is underneath the stands, tucked away below ground level and surrounded with concrete. There's little or no available cell phone service, and so it was common all afternoon and into the evening for reporters to wander the halls and climb to the concourses, calling hospital spokespeople and Kent Brown in an effort to answer the key questions: How was Dawn Weber? And would her son coach his team in Saturday's semifinal against Minnesota?

It wasn't the sort of news Kent Brown had gotten into the business to deal with. And yet, it was the kind of thing he'd grown painfully accustomed to over the course of the year. In August, Brown had lost his wife, Robin, to cancer. Six months later, his father passed away. For all the magic of 2004-05, it had been a taxing year for Kent, and for his children, daughter Nicholle and son Ty.

"A lot of people spend an inordinate amount of time and money to follow Illinois basketball and want to be a part of it," Brown would later say. "To the coaches and our staff, it's important. But you realize there are things out there in life that exceed the importance of basketball."

By the end of the day, Brown was dealing with one of those things again. Price and Webster were scouting the Iowa-Michigan State game that night when a Big Ten representative asked them to come to a room in the hallways beneath the United Center.

"I don't have a pen," Price said as he walked off press row.

"You won't need one," he was told.

That's when Price and Webster learned that Dawn Weber had died that night, during heart surgery. Before long, the rest of the United Center would find out, too.

Decision Time

At Rush University Medical Center, Bruce Weber and his family still were making calls, trying to reach family and friends to deliver the heartbreaking news. But there was no controlling the story, and before long, it seemed, half the United Center was aware. When Kent Brown circulated word through the press room, the place was hushed. And when reporters walked out to catch the end of Iowa's win against Michigan State, fans yelled from the stands asking for updates.

"One of the worst things," Price said, "was that word was getting out before [Weber] wanted it to."

Not everyone had been reached, and the Weber family still was scrambling to tell relatives over the phone before they learned on the Big Ten tournament broadcast that Dawn Weber had died. When that task finally was completed, there was another issue to address. Back at Rush, talk had turned to basketball. While his mother was in surgery, David Weber had left the hospital to coach his Glenbrook North High School team in a sectional game. He'd received word of his mother's passing by cell phone in the postgame locker room. Sixteen teenagers had engulfed him in a hug, their emotions on overdrive after a 37-36 win.

Now it was up to Bruce Weber to decide if he would coach his team after his mother's death. In truth, the decision wasn't difficult.

"It's what she would've wanted," Weber said later. "She loved basketball, loved for us to coach. She was so proud of both of our teams. She wouldn't have wanted me to miss a game."

A Long Night

At the team hotel, players were doing their best to stick to their normal routines. There was a team meeting without Weber, who had called to tell his staff to inform the players that he would coach. Meanwhile, McClain scrambled to complete the Minnesota scouting report, an adventure in itself. Preparing a scouting report during the regular season can be a frantic process, but during the postseason, with so little time, it's even more challenging. McClain, as always, had taken copious notes during Minnesota's afternoon game. He'd watched film on the Gophers prior to the game. And he had a legal pad loaded with strategies and tendencies that needed to be typed and printed. In theory, that was a simple process.

McClain and head manager Matt McCumber walked a few blocks to a nearby Kinko's so that McCumber could type McClain's notes into a scouting report and the two could bring back copies for each player and coach. But after what seemed like a long walk on a bitter cold night, the two were turned away.

"They were closed, and they sent us to another Kinko's," McCumber said. That Kinko's was also was closed. "It was unreal," McCumber said. "When does Kinko's ever close?"

The two ended up taking a cab to a cross-town Kinko's and completing the scouting report in time for that night's meeting, which went as well as could be expected. Players were focused on Minnesota the next day, but their thoughts also were with Weber, across town at the hospital, still mourning and already making funeral arrangements.

"When he hurts," Dee Brown said, "we all hurt."

Illinois' players—talented and driven though they were—always had a tendency to drift off during prolonged scouting reports, and their attentiveness in 2004-05, Weber would often say, was a key in the transition from a good team to a great one. Still, the coaching staff wondered what they'd get that night when the players filed into the hotel meeting room. What they received was consistent with the rest of the year: A college team that carried itself like consummate professionals.

"Our guys were amazing," Price said. "Of course they were distracted. Of course their hearts weren't in it like they could be, because they were thinking of Coach Weber. But one thing we knew with this group was that they would be focused even though Coach Weber wasn't there."

Despite Weber's absence, the coaching staff wanted the players' night to be as normal as possible. They had a team meal and the team meeting and then went to their rooms. Roger Powell Jr., the licensed minister, led the team in prayer, and Powell himself prayed several times that night. Powell's teammates went about their nightly routines—playing video games in their rooms, mostly—while the support staff was hard at work.

There was more scouting to be done and more film to watch in preparation for the game. And though that was on the night's agenda, the assistant coaches also thought to tell Rod Cardinal to work on getting a black band added to the Illini's uniforms in memory of Dawn Weber. Illinois' cheerleaders were hard at work, too, putting together lapel pins with flowers and orange ribbon that they'd present to the coaches the next day. By gametime, the entire Illinois staff—Bruce Weber included—would have one pinned on. Weber arrived at the hotel late, but in time to meet with his staff and discuss the next day's game.

"It was a hard night, for all of us," Price said. "Just to see him break down, it was really emotional."

Welcome Back, Coach

Back at the United Center on Saturday morning, Weber's arrival was as anticipated as a president's. Television cameras lined up in the tunnel where Illinois would enter the arena from its team bus. And when Weber walked in, their lights came alive. The coach, clearly exhausted, kept his head down as he headed down the hallway—literally lined on both sides with reporters—to a small room the Big Ten had set up for his family to meet. He gave a brief interview to ESPN's Erin Andrews, then went to meet his team.

When he did, Jack Ingram spoke for his teammates. Along with Brown and Williams, Ingram had become a vocal leader in the locker room, and he gladly accepted the role.

"I just wanted to really convey our support for him," Ingram said. "He had a tough loss in his family, and we just wanted to thank him for being able to come and coach us and lead us, and just really express our condolences."

It was the first in a string of emotional moments for Weber. The next would be almost too much to take. The crowd reaction—a long, loud ovation that came largely from the overwhelming majority of fans who were in orange—began when Weber first walked out on the court. But the rest of the crowd joined in, too, fans from

Wisconsin and Michigan State and Minnesota standing to applaud the Illinois coach. An Illinois fan held up a sign that read, "*Saddened By Your Loss, Inspired By Your Courage.*"

But the most heartfelt moment came just before the game, after the introduction of the starting lineups. The United Center's public address announcer asked for a moment of silence in memory of Dawn Weber. After the moment, the United Center erupted, an outpouring of emotion that moved Weber to tears.

"It was overwhelming," Weber said. "It really was touching."

And then each of Minnesota's players—and Goldy, the school's Gopher mascot—approached Weber to shake his hand. He fought back tears then, too.

"I think the fact that the Minnesota kids did that," Price said, "was really special to him."

Even more powerful was what his team would do for Weber.

All-out, All Day

A truckload of awards is presented every year at Illinois' postseason banquet. There are awards for free throw shooting and leadership and a most valuable player honor that's put up to a team vote. None of them means quite as much as the "Matto." The Matto Award, given since 2002, honors the player who plays the hardest. There's a formula to determine the winner, based mostly on deflections and charges taken, and since Dee Brown set foot on campus, he's owned the thing. And yet, each time he's won it, Brown has been moved. When Lucas Johnson won the Matto his senior year, he broke down in tears accepting it.

To anyone who's played at Illinois, the Matto means more than a plaque. The award is named for Matt "Matto" Heldman, a guard on Illinois' 1998 Big Ten championship team. Known for his all-out hustle and desire, Heldman had turned himself into a contributor by sheer force of will. Though hardly the most talented kid, he was as beloved as anyone who ever put on the uniform. In 1999, Matt Heldman was killed in an October car accident near his hometown of Libertyville, Illinois. The Orange Krush had established—and ultimately endowed—a scholarship in Heldman's honor, and the Matto Award was created to honor his memory.

"When I watched Illinois games, I remember him from his three-point shooting and his hard work," Brown said. "It's good for me to carry on his name and go out there and try to play my game, the way he used to play."

These days, Weber's staff has managers chart "Matto" points during games. On March 12, it was hard to keep up. The emotion of the day played out on the court, and the Illini were rocky early that day against Minnesota. They shot 34.5 percent in the first half and 35.7 percent for the game, and they committed a season-high 23 turnovers. But Illinois' gritty defense made sure that the Gophers struggled just as mightily. In the process, the Illini set a season high on the Matto chart.

"I think that was a reflection of them playing for me," Weber said. "To see that the whole thing had an impact on them really meant a lot."

In the end, Illinois won a 64-56 slugfest, with Augustine again putting in a workmanlike effort with 11 points and 14 rebounds. After the game, Augustine was the first to find his coach and wrap a long arm around his shoulder. And rather than look back with emotion, Augustine looked ahead with excitement. "We got one more, Coach," he told Weber. It was just what the coach wanted to hear.

A Return to Normal

After the Minnesota game, Weber and his team did their best to get back to normalcy. The coach skipped his typical post-press conference meeting with the media, instead meeting behind closed doors with his family to discuss funeral arrangements. But he tried to stay involved over the course of the day—with scouting, with meetings—in an attempt to get back into the routine.

"We all just hoped that maybe basketball would take his mind off things for a few hours at a time," Ingram said. And it did.

"There's no doubt at that point, basketball was all that kept me going," Weber said. "I was just trying to survive."

His team, meanwhile, had a renewed focus to accomplish its third goal of the season. With a perfect pre-conference slate and a Big Ten title wrapped up, the Illini wanted to beat Wisconsin in the Big Ten tournament final to win their second postseason title in three years. It promised to be no easy feat. Since its 70-59 loss at Illinois in February, Wisconsin had lost just once, at Michigan State. And in the games leading up to the tournament title matchup, the Badgers had looked like a team of destiny. Alando Tucker had beaten Indiana in the regular season's final week with a buzzer-beating putback. And in the Big Ten tournament semifinal, Tucker banked in a 25-foot three-pointer at the buzzer to beat Iowa, 59-56.

There's an adage in basketball that states that it's never easy to beat a team three times in a season. It figured to be even more challenging against a shrewd coach like Bo Ryan, who was facing an Illinois team that might be fatigued, not just physically but mentally. The statistics would indicate that things didn't come easily for the Illini. Dee Brown shot zero for eight from the floor. Deron Williams was three for 10. Numbers like that don't typically bode well for Illinois. But just in the nick of time, there was Augustine again.

The junior forward—whom Weber had pushed as a first-team All-Big Ten candidate, but who had been left off the first-team ballots—came into the tournament "with a little bit of a chip on his shoulder," Weber said. And it showed. Against the Badgers in a grind-it-out title game, he had 12 points and nine rebounds. He made all five of his shots. And he swatted away three of the Badgers' attempts.

"He kind of intimidated our guys a little bit," Ryan said.

Powell, too, had gone to work, scoring 15 points and grabbing 12 rebounds. More importantly, in a game that Illinois dominated with its defense, Augustine and Powell combined to silence first-team All-Big Ten selection Mike Wilkinson. The Wisconsin center managed just eight points, six of them on free throws, and shot one for seven from the floor.

After the game—a 54-43 win in which Illinois was rarely threatened—the players slid Big Ten tournament championship T-shirts on over their jerseys and donned championship hats. They snipped the nets and basked in the thunderous applause that rained down

The Illini celebrate with the Big Ten Tournament championship trophy after defeating Wisconsin 54-43. *Robert K. O'Daniell/The News-Gazette*

from the rafters of the United Center. As Augustine watched Big Ten commissioner Jim Delany hand out hardware, he chatted with roommate Nick Smith. The NCAA tournament selection show was due to start soon, and the Illini would watch from a restaurant in the United Center.

"I wonder what they're going to have to eat?," Augustine asked Smith. That's when he heard his name announced as the tournament's MVP. "I had no idea that was coming," Augustine said.

Shortly thereafter, Weber took the microphone to thank Illinois fans for their support, and though he'd addressed crowds before, this time was different. Still punch-drunk from a flood of emotions, Weber smiled and shook his head in near-disbelief as fans moaned, "Bruuuuuuuuuce."

"We have a good problem," Weber told the crowd. "We're running out of places to put trophies in our office."

But there was only one he really wanted. And—finally—it was time to chase it.

10

ON TO THE MADNESS

The Illini felt good heading into the NCAA tournament. Though their offense had struggled in the regular-season finale against Ohio State and in the Big Ten tournament—Dee Brown had missed 18 of his last 23 three-point attempts—the defense had been stellar. And when the backcourt had struggled, the frontcourt had picked up the slack.

On the Monday before the NCAA tournament was to begin, Illinois players met the media before practice. Standing in the hallway outside the Ubben Basketball Complex's men's practice court, we watched as Brown warmed up for practice by launching three-pointers. We watched as Brown drilled 14 straight, breaking a sweat but never a smile. The Illini were content to have won the Big Ten tournament with their defense. But the goal was to get offensive again, to get clicking from three-point range, and to get the guards and the big men on the same page offensively.

"If we can do that," Deron Williams said, "we're going to be pretty tough to stop."

They figured to be a pretty tough match early on regardless. Illinois, the overall No. 1 seed in the tournament, had drawn Fairleigh Dickinson in the first round, and the Illini would play their first- and second-round games in Indianapolis, about a two-hour drive from Champaign. All season, Weber's mantra to the team had been "Get on the bus," his catchphrase for motivating his players to secure a No. 1 seed. In doing so, Illinois had guaranteed itself the rarest of NCAA tournament runs. The Illini could advance all the way to the Final Four in St. Louis without ever boarding a plane. Their first two games would be in Indianapolis. Win those, and it was on to Rosemont, just outside Chicago, a little more than a two-hour drive from campus. St. Louis was just three hours away.

"We talked about it all year," James Augustine said. "We kept saying that was the path we wanted. Really, we were talking about it since the end of last year."

After Illinois had lost to Duke in the Sweet 16 in 2004, Weber had immediately discussed the 2005 Final Four with his team. Pictures of St. Louis went up in the Illinois locker room, and Weber established right away that the team's goals in 2004-05 should be nothing short of college basketball's pinnacle. To get there, though, the Illini first had to win a couple of games in Indianapolis.

Fairleigh Dickinson shaped up to be a pushover. But the second-round matchup—against the winner of the Texas vs. Nevada game—was a potential early speed bump. Illinois was aware that anything short of a Final Four run would be a disappointment to its fans, but it wasn't easy to get them to talk about it.

"They won't be any more disappointed than we will," Brown said.

Orange You from Champaign?

The debate the first two days of the NCAA's opening week centered on who would bring the most fans to Indianapolis. Illinois had been sent to Indy as the No. 1 seed in the Chicago Regional, and Illini fans had been planning their tournament route for a year. As the nation's No. 1 team and the odds-on favorite to win the national championship, Illinois presumed to bring a good chunk of Champaign-Urbana on the trip.

But mighty Kentucky, too? They would open the tournament in Indianapolis as the No. 2 seed in the Austin Regional. There would be no chance for the Illini and Wildcats to play, but there was a rivalry there nonetheless. Kentucky would open against Eastern Kentucky, and a possible matchup against nearby Cincinnati awaited in the second round. And with Wildcat fans famous for their postseason travel, they were expected to make the three-hour drive from Lexington, Kentucky, in droves.

As it turned out, it wasn't even close. Kentucky did bring legions of fans to Indianapolis, and they filed into the RCA Dome for the open practice day decked out in their royal blue and white. But the Illinois fans were overwhelming. They arrived early for the open practices, chanting "ILL-INI" and roaring at the introduction of their beloved team.

"It feels like home," Illinois forward Warren Carter said.

Fairleigh Confident

Meanwhile, Fairleigh Dickinson's players were saying all the right things, confident that they could overcome Illinois' crowd, certain that they could give the Illini a game. No one much believed them. But maybe they should've.

The game started about as it was expected to, with a boisterous Illinois crowd cheering its team on to an early seven-point lead. But the Knights were getting good looks from inside and missing clean attempts from three-point range. When shots began to fall, Fairleigh Dickinson made a run, at one point rallying from that seven-point deficit to take the lead. Illinois led by four in the closing seconds of the first half when Tamien Trent provided the Knights one final spark. The FDU point guard fired up a three-pointer at the halftime buzzer that swished to cut Illinois' lead to a scant—and stunning—32-31. And as he ran back toward the locker room, Trent looped his thumbs under his jersey and tugged so that everyone could see his school's name on the front, a gesture clearly intended to mock Brown's trademark move.

"It didn't make me real happy," Brown said.

Boiling Point

There is a pattern to an Illinois halftime, as with most teams. The Illinois players sit alone in the locker room for five minutes, give or take, while the coaching staff meets in a hallway or separate room to discuss the halftime talking points. While the players wait-

Dee Brown was less than thrilled with Fairleigh Dickinson's cocky attitude. In the second half, the Illini pulled away for a 67-55 victory. Brown finished the game with a team-high 19 points. *Elsa/Getty Images*

ed for the coaches to enter at halftime of the FDU game, they steamed and stewed.

"Angry," Deron Williams responded when asked to describe the mood. "Embarrassed."

Weber didn't need to give a rah-rah speech. So he didn't. He told his players simply that he was disappointed.

"We'd had a tendency all year to maybe let up or relax against teams without a great reputation," Weber said. "I just told them I was disappointed that they would do that at the NCAA tournament."

His message didn't peel paint. He didn't throw anything. He didn't have to. Illinois responded with its defense, harassing the Knights into turnovers while holding Fairleigh Dickinson to 31-percent shooting in the second half—after a sizzling 50 percent in the first. The Illini scored 14 of the first 16 points in the second half, and though the knockout punch never came, Fairleigh Dickinson was never a threat. Illinois won 67-55.

Afterward the Knights said they weren't impressed with Brown, Illinois' best-known player, and that they were disappointed that they hadn't become the first 16th-seeded team in NCAA history to knock off a No. 1. They weren't the only ones unimpressed. The Illini weren't very pleased with themselves, either.

"Thank God we got it out of the way now," Roger Powell Jr. said. "We've got to pick it up next game and play Illinois basketball the way we're capable of playing."

Nick of Time

That next game would come two days later against Nevada, the No. 9 seed in the Chicago Regional, which had pulled a mild upset of eighth-seeded Texas in Indianapolis the day Illinois outlasted Fairleigh Dickinson. The Wolf Pack had made an NCAA tournament splash the year before when guard Kirk Snyder led the team to the Sweet 16. But Snyder had entered the NBA draft, and Nevada in 2004-05 was a young team considered a year ahead of schedule. The Wolf Pack had reached the tournament—and the second round—largely thanks to sophomore center Nick Fazekas, a versatile six-foot-11 player who had been named Player of the Year in the Western Athletic Conference.

The guess was that slowing Fazekas would be Illinois' top priority. But Weber had other ideas. As he had been all year, Weber was more concerned with his own team than with the competition. So he sought a way to motivate his team, to push the right buttons to get the Illini back into the groove. That motivation came from multiple sources. First, Weber asked his team if it had watched North Carolina's first-round game. The Tar Heels had routed Oakland 96-68, had won the way a top seed is expected to win in the opening round.

"Did anybody see Carolina play at the beginning of the game?" Weber asked, knowing well that his team had seen the game. "Guys are diving into the stands, they're making plays, screaming, yelling. We haven't had that. We need to do that."

During the season, Illinois had grown tired of the constant comparisons to the Tar Heels. Weber was hoping that drawing a comparison himself—a negative one at that—might light a fire under his players. My newspaper helped stoke that flame. For every game, I do a preview graphic for *The News-Gazette*, an informative box that's expanded to almost a full page for the NCAA tournament. At tournament time, it includes a position-by-position breakdown. For the Nevada game, I gave Fazekas the edge over Augustine. Fazekas was the Wolf Pack's best player, I figured. He was a matchup nightmare, I thought. He had the potential to cause real problems. But the Illini got Saturday's paper at the hotel and read it during breakfast. And immediately, that simple preview box became a motivational tool.

"That doesn't bother me," Augustine would say later, but his teammates begged to differ. They'd pointed out the slight to him. They'd ridden him about it a little, too. And they saw a fire light in his eyes.

"I think he thought it was disrespect," Williams said.

"If you have pride," Weber said, "you want to show you can compete with anybody."

Augustine certainly showed that he could compete with Fazekas. The Illinois junior had 23 points and 10 rebounds and

Perhaps some additional motivation from *The News-Gazette* pushed James Augustine on to a career night against Nevada in Round 2 of the NCAA tournament. The junior center put an exclamation point on Illinois' 71-59 win over the Wolfpack by scoring 23 points and grabbing 10 rebounds.
Darrell Hoemann/The News-Gazette

helped hold the WAC Player of the Year to 11 points on five-for-20 shooting, and Illinois blew out Nevada 71-59 in a game that never felt close. When Augustine broke loose for an early two-handed dunk, he snapped the rim and let loose with a scream that did his coaches proud. It was a joyful scream—a Carolina scream.

"We looked like our old selves," guard Luther Head said. "We were having fun."

But the fun was just beginning.

Family, Friends and a Foe

Illinois players were ecstatic to advance, naturally, but the chance to play in—or at least near—Chicago was an added bonus. Though the Illini's Sweet 16 and Elite Eight games would be played in Rosemont, near the O'Hare airport and a considerable drive from downtown Chicago, it meant that the families of in-state players would have an easy trip.

Not that it would have mattered to most of them. Take, for example, Dale Augustine. Through the first three seasons of his son's Illinois career, Dale hadn't missed a game. Not the ones in Vegas. Not the ones in New York. Not even the ones in Champaign when blinding snow plagued the roads between the family's home in Mokena, Illinois, and the Illinois campus.

"I've told him before that he doesn't have to come," James Augustine said of his dad. "But I think he just likes to be at all the games. It's cool. I mean, it's nice that he wants to support me."

As a high school teacher and assistant football coach, Dale Augustine's nights and weekends are free during the basketball season. And when he's had to take a personal day or two, his employers have been understanding. Not every parent has that luxury, but the parents of Illinois' in-state players still made every effort. Cathy Brown-Blocker was there during the tournament run, too, sporting her son's No. 11 jersey. And Bonnie Gallion, Luther Head's mother, came in her son's No. 4, often waving an Illinois pompon and cheering every play.

"It means everything," Head said. "It's special when your family can see you play. That's why you want to go to school in-state to begin with. That's why having the tournament so close is great."

But family members wouldn't be the only friendly faces at the Allstate Arena in Rosemont. Unlike the cavernous RCA Dome, which held more than 40,000 fans for the first two rounds of NCAA play, Allstate would accommodate fewer than 17,000, and Illinois fans, hoping for a year that their team would be playing for a Final Four berth in the Chicago area, were expected to have most of those tickets.

The Illini Nation was expected to show up with vigor—and venom—because Illinois' Sweet 16 game in Rosemont would pit the Illini against one of the most notorious figures in the program's 100 years of basketball history. As an assistant coach at Iowa in the early 1990s, Bruce Pearl had secretly taped phone conversations with high school recruit Deon Thomas, in which Thomas told Pearl he'd been given cash and a car to attend Illinois. Thomas later insisted that he was only joking, that he'd told Pearl what he wanted to hear to get the Iowa assistant off the phone. But Pearl's recordings would lead to an NCAA investigation. And though no evidence of cash payments to Thomas was found, and though the Chevy Blazer he told Pearl he'd been given was never produced, Illinois landed on NCAA probation.

In announcing a one-year postseason ban for the basketball program, the NCAA's Chuck Smrt famously remarked, "Just because they weren't found guilty doesn't mean they didn't do it." Other allegations had been made, and the NCAA took a "where there's smoke there's fire approach," slapping Illinois with a lack of institutional control charge.

By the time the 2004-05 tournament began, it had been 13 years since Illinois had been forced to sit out the NCAA tournament. And given the program's successes since, one might logically think that Illinois fans would have moved on. But it wasn't that simple. The Illini faithful felt that Pearl's actions—on the heels of the 1989 Final Four—derailed a program that had unprecedented momentum. And the grudge wasn't going away. Pearl had become persona non grata in Illinois. He had left Iowa, then worked his way up through the coaching ranks—some felt that he'd been blacklist-ed for years after his handling of the Thomas case—to eventually build a solid mid-major program at the University of Wisconsin-Milwaukee.

That was the school he would lead into the Sweet Sixteen against Illinois. It also happened to be Bruce Weber's alma mater. The irony was lost on the Illini ("They didn't know where I went to college until you guys told them," Weber told me), and so was the impact of the Pearl case. They'd been made aware of fans' disdain for Pearl, usually around the time the Iowa games rolled around every year, but it had mostly gone in one ear and out the other.

"I don't even know why we're talking about this," Brown said. "It was 15 years ago. It doesn't mean anything to me or to any of us or to anybody on Wisconsin-Milwaukee. This is about the people playing now—us against them."

Illinois fans weren't so sure. This was a man whom many of them—judging by the calls and e-mails I received at *The News-Gazette*—truly hated Pearl, a man with whom University of Illinois-Chicago coach Jimmy Collins (an assistant at Illinois during Pearl's days at Iowa) still didn't shake hands. Forgetting was hard. Forgiving was impossible.

Head Hamstrung

Media—and Allstate Arena security—expected the greeting for Pearl to be brutal, and the Milwaukee coach was prepared for it.

"Do you think, no matter who was going in there to play Illinois, the coach would get cheered?" Pearl asked. "Now, is it going to be a little worse for me because of all the things that happened? It probably is."

But Pearl steadfastly declined to talk in detail about the Thomas situation, and Weber wanted to avoid it as well. He didn't use it as a motivational tactic with his team. Knowing that reporters would ask questions about it, the Illinois media relations staff had given the players a "CliffsNotes" version of the Thomas affair; but as gameday approached, the story became a subplot to the game, which would be Illinois' first against a trapping, full-court pressure team since a December date with Arkansas.

Soon enough, Illinois had more pressing concerns. I had missed Illinois' shootaround that afternoon, instead spending my time interviewing Pearl and his players in preparation for Thursday's game. Unaware that Head was in pain, I'd conducted my interviews of both teams and written my stories for Thursday's paper. Late on Wednesday night, after I'd returned to my hotel room next door to Allstate Arena, I got a call from Travis Drury.

Drury was an Illinois student, a member of the Orange Krush and an on-air personality at student-run radio station WPGU 107.1-FM. He'd seen a broadcast report indicating Head was injured and might not play against Milwaukee. He wanted to know what I'd heard. And I'd heard nothing. Though it was late—about 11:30 p.m.—I went back to work. I tried to reach Illinois' sports information staff first, but struck out with both Kent Brown and Derrick Burson. So I called Jay Price on his cell phone. And the assistant coach assured me that Head was fine.

"He's going to play tomorrow," he said.

Reassured, I hung up my cell phone. Minutes later, it rang. The number on my caller ID was Price's.

"Brett," Bruce Weber's voice squawked. "It's Coach. Jay's a liar."

Weber had been in the room when I'd called Price. And though the "liar" comment was an exaggeration, intended as a joke, Weber admitted that there was more to the story. And he was going to tell me. But not before he had a little fun.

"Luther tore up his knee—he's done," Weber said, clearly joking. "Also, we're going to start Nick Smith and Rich McBride, and we're going to play a 2-3 zone. Doesn't that sound like a good strategy?"

After a good laugh, Weber leveled with me, saying that Head had tweaked his hamstring during a practice earlier in the week. He could run, but not comfortably.

"We think he'll play," Weber said. "But you never know with those things."

I got the story into my office in time for Thursday's first edition.

Pearl Payback

Allstate Arena held 16,957 fans for the Chicago Regional games, but the place seemed smaller than that. It's old wooden ceiling seemed like something out of the movie *Hoosiers*, and there was an almost palpable energy in the cramped little building that felt like the juice that fills the Assembly Hall for an Illinois home game. Maybe that had something to do with the overwhelming majority of fans in orange. Estimates put the crowd at about 80 percent Illinois fans on the first night, with fans from Milwaukee, Arizona, and Oklahoma State fighting for scraps. And in a confined space with a low roof, that 80 percent made enough noise to have been 80,000.

John Brumbaugh sat in that crowd, a bundle of nervous energy. Brumbaugh had become something of a celebrity in the Illinois basketball community. An Illinois grad, he had launched the Web site IlliniBoard.com, the No. 1 Internet message board for Illini fans. I'd written a story about him a few years before, and we'd become friends, swapping stories and trading rumors during the season.

"I don't know what I'll do if we lose," he'd told me the day before the game. "I'll probably just sit there with a big hole in my chest, because Bruce Pearl will have ripped my heart out."

It was a common sentiment among the Illinois faithful, as evidenced by the hearty boos that rained down on Pearl, first when he took the court for warmups and again when he was introduced by the public-address announcer. Soon enough, though, Illini fans had something to cheer.

Milwaukee played at a furious pace, and Pearl had promised not to back down from Illinois' new "Flyin' Illini." He didn't. For the first 10 minutes, the game was played at a breakneck pace, with both teams running the court and trading big plays. Though they shot 53 percent in the first half, the Illini led by only seven, and with its ability to score in spurts, Wisconsin-Milwaukee was hardly out of the game.

Illinois pulled away early in the second half and led by as many as 17, but Joah Tucker, who scored 32 points for the Panthers, helped keep the game close. And though the Illini controlled the second half, it wasn't as comfortable as the 77-63 final score indicated.

"I was looking at the clock with like seven minutes to go," said Williams, who tied Brown for a team-best 21 points, "and I swear I didn't think it was ever going to move again."

Afterward, Arizona took the court and—thanks to Salim Stoudamire's clutch jumper—beat Oklahoma State 79-78. The Wildcats looked like a serious threat, but the Illini had already had enough "serious." Despite what the players had said publicly, there had been pressure not to lose to Pearl, not to let a man Illini fans loathed above all others end the school's most magical season. Their victory over Pearl was another in a string of weights lifted off of Illinois' shoulders.

In the postgame press conference, Brown handed Weber a cup of water. As he did, he whispered, just loud enough for the microphone to pick it up, "I put my finger in it." Everybody laughed.

The Illini were back. Now they wanted back in the Final Four.

11

THE GAME OF
THE CENTURY

Even as Michigan State and Wisconsin were doing the Big Ten proud in other NCAA tournament regions, there were questions about Illinois and its capability to win a big game against a team as talented as Arizona, its Elite Eight opponent. The consensus all season had been that, while Illinois was undoubtedly great, it had beaten up on weaker competition throughout the conference season. And the general feeling was that it had been months—since perhaps the Wake Forest game—since Illinois had played a team the caliber of Arizona.

How would Illinois respond to that challenge? How would the Illini react to a tight game at crunch time? And how was Head's health? Those were the questions on everyone's mind. And there were plenty of people asking them. On the Friday afternoon between Illinois' win against Milwaukee and its game against the Wildcats, the media contingent at Allstate Arena was enormous, and there was little room for it. A record-setting number of reporters had followed the Illini through the first and second rounds and on to the Sweet 16, and in Rosemont it became increasingly difficult to find any space in which to interview the Illini. The locker room was cramped and overcrowded—so much so that when the horde of reporters had come in after the Milwaukee game, players who had-n't played significant roles left their lockers to provide more breathing room for their in-demand teammates.

The day before the Arizona game, Illinois' five starters were taken to interview "breakout rooms," which in most venues are actual rooms, but in Rosemont were makeshift cubicles made of metal piping draped with fabric, indoor tents of sorts. When Luther Head was asked a question in his breakout room, his soft voice was barely audible over the more boisterous Brown, whose own press conference was separated only by a thin blue curtain. But the questions—and answers—were the same no matter which room you entered. Would the Illini have what it took to withstand this kind of test, and how would they stop Stoudamire, college basketball's more accurate three-point shooter and the man who'd buried Oklahoma State?

"We're just excited to play," said Williams, who would draw the assignment of guarding Stoudamire. "We've waited all year for this, the chance to get this program back in the Final Four."

They would need Head to do it, and the prognosis, if not perfect, was good. He'd received treatment well into the night after the Milwaukee game, and the same plan would follow the night before the Arizona game. Head would be ready. The Illini promised they would, too. If the pressure was getting to them—they'd known all season that anything short of a Final Four appearance would be considered a bust—then the Illini weren't showing it. They looked loose. They looked confident. But so did Arizona.

Outside Influences

If Illinois fans everywhere were pulling for the Illini to make it past the Wildcats, some notable ones in Rosemont were providing added motivation. Like most of his hometown, Chicagoan Bill Murray had jumped on the Illinois bandwagon, and he had asked to speak to the team, a request Weber had happily granted. Among entertainment journalists, Murray has a reputation for being difficult. He snaps at questions he doesn't want to answer, or clams up entirely during interviews. But Illinois players and coaches saw an entirely different side of Murray. He laughed. He told jokes. When Dee Brown asked him to give a part of his speech to the Illini in

Broadcaster Loren Tate (left) shares a laugh with actor Bill Murray (right) during the Arizona game. Murray was one of many celebrities who took a liking to the Illini in 2004–05. *John Dixon/The News-Gazette*

character as Carl Spackler, the half-wit he'd played in the movie *Caddyshack* 25 years before, Murray obliged.

"He was just hilarious," said Weber, who chatted with Murray a number of times in Rosemont. "Just like you'd expect him to be if you've seen his movies. He's just one of those guys who, everything he says is funny."

Murray was the biggest celebrity to speak to Illinois that weekend, but not the only one. Weber also had former Illini Kendall Gill, a starter on Illinois' last Final Four team in 1989, address the team in the locker room. Gill had played 14 years in the NBA, his basketball career only recently having ended, but the speech he gave to the players wasn't about the wealth he amassed during his playing days.

"The feeling I had in college, going to the Final Four, that was something I never got back," Gill said. "I never had the same kind of experience again. You have the opportunity to have that experience now. Take advantage of it, because you never know when you'll have a chance like this again."

Another Rival

Illinois fans didn't have the same disdain for Arizona's Lute Olson that they reserved for Wisconsin-Milwaukee's Bruce Pearl, but there still was ire there. Olson and the Wildcats had ended the Illini's last Elite Eight trip in 2001 in a foul-plagued game that saw six Illinois players foul out. Fans still claimed that Olson's pregame politicking—he had called Illinois' Lucas Johnson "dirty" in addressing the press—had played a factor in the referees' calling of the game.

Many Illinois fans began to look at the 2005 NCAA tournament as an opportunity, not only to reach the Final Four, but to exorcise demons along the way: first Pearl, then Arizona. Given that, and Illinois' decided home-state advantage, it was no surprise that Illini fans had bought up most of the tickets for sale by fans from Wisconsin-Milwaukee and Oklahoma State.

"It felt like the Assembly Hall in that place, with all of our fans," James Augustine said.

Illinois would need every last one of them.

Let the Game Begin

From the outset, it was clear that Arizona was a different brand of team than those Illinois had seen lately, perhaps all season. Long, fast, and athletic, the Wildcats had a typical roster for the powerhouse from the Pac-10 Conference: stocked with NBA caliber-talent, and enigmatic enough to struggle against an also-ran but come to play against a powerhouse.

Against Illinois, Arizona came to play. The Wildcats weren't phased by the crowd, nor by Illinois' gaudy 34-1 record, nor by the early lead the Illini built in the second half. Stoudamire was struggling to find his shot, but Hassan Adams was off to a strong start, and Channing Frye—who would go on to be a first-round pick of the NBA's New York Knicks—was terrorizing the Illini inside.

Illinois led 38-36 at the half, but Arizona had all the momentum. The Wildcats had closed the half on a strong run, and as they sprinted off the court, it was with supreme confidence. They had shot 52 percent from the floor and they trailed by only two. Arizona had reason to believe. Soon enough, Illinois would have virtually none.

"They came out in the second half, and we just couldn't stop them," Weber said. "Every shot was going in. Every bounce was going their way."

And every Illinois run was swatted down. Arizona grabbed the lead early, then stretched it, first to six points, then to double digits. And then the Cats pushed it out some more. Frye was dominant, scoring inside and out on his way to 24 points. He even dropped in a three-pointer that took the energy out of the orange-clad Illinois fans. With four minutes to play, Arizona led 75-60. You could've heard a pin drop if not for the traditional chant from the small pack of Arizona fans behind press row and sprinkled throughout the arena: "Bear Down!"

Preparing for the Finish

Sitting in his 100 level seat at Allstate Arena, John Brumbaugh had seen enough. The longtime Illinois fan stood up, walked upstairs to a 200 level seat, and buried his head in his hands.

"This is the life of an Illinois fan," Brumbaugh thought. "It can't end this way. These guys were supposed to be the ones who got it done, and they're not going to do it." He could hardly look up.

A level below on press row, I began to prepare an "obit," short for obituary. As insensitive as it might sound, that's the phrase sportswriters sometimes use to describe the end of a season. The season dies, and it's your job to administer its last rites. Throughout the NCAA tournament, *The News-Gazette* had staffed each game with four other writers, and each of them had their assignments in the case of an Illinois win. We hadn't produced a plan for a loss. Our sports editor, Jim Rossow, had been certain Illinois would beat Arizona. We hadn't spent much time planning for the alternative.

As the beat writer, it was my job to produce an "obit" plan. So I began scribbling assignments and story suggestions for our other writers in attendance: Bob Asmussen, Tony Bleill, and Jeff Mezydlo, as well as thoughts for Loren Tate, the paper's longtime columnist who also was working the radio broadcast with Brian Barnhart and Steve Bardo. We call the next day's story plan a "budget," and I still have that obit budget, in a box of things I kept from the season. I was certain then that I'd be putting it to use.

On the Illinois bench, they were only slightly less certain of the outcome. There was little life among the players sitting to Bruce Weber's left. All season, redshirts Brian Randle and Calvin Brock had been Illinois' loudest cheerleaders. With the clock showing a little more than four minutes remaining in the game, however, they were mostly silent.

At the end of the bench, student manager Matt McCumber was quiet, too. A senior, McCumber had grown up a diehard Illinois fan in Tuscola, a small town just outside Champaign. As he watched his favorite team headed for what looked like certain defeat, he was nostalgic. "It's been a great run," McCumber thought. "I've had four great years. Two Elite Eights. Got a few rings. Met a lot of great people." McCumber didn't want to give up. He was merely bracing for the inevitable. The rest of the Illinois fans in Rosemont and around the country were doing the same. And so were the Wildcats.

With a little more than four minutes to play, Adams had turned to Stoudamire and said, "Five minutes to St. Louis," trying hard to hold back a smile. And as Arizona pulled away, the Allstate Arena staff quickly and quietly emerged from the tunnel with cardboard boxes to place behind the Wildcats' bench.

Sealed up in those boxes were the "Chicago Regional Champions" T-shirts and hats that had been printed up for the Wildcats. They'd never make it out of the box.

One Last Gasp

Ask anyone involved—player, coach, fan, or reporter—and they'll tell you the next four minutes of game time were a blur. Weber gave impassioned speeches in timeout huddles, but no one can remember them. Illinois players screamed encouragement at each other, but no one can say what the exact words were. In fact, the only piece of dialogue anyone admits to remembering is what Brown told Williams late in the game.

"You're the best guard in the country," Brown said. "You're going to dominate down the stretch."

But it's hard to think that Brown actually believed there was still hope for the Illini, even as Illinois was whittling away at Arizona's lead. Luther Head's three-pointer started the rally, but it seemed too little too late. Brown scored in the paint, but it still felt like little more than part of a run to respectability. Then Arizona started to turn the ball over. And the tide started turning, too. Head scored off a steal, and Jeremy Rutherford, then the Illinois beat writer for the *St. Louis Post-Dispatch* turned to me and said, "A couple more baskets, and this is a game," but neither of us was ready to scrap our season-ending story ideas yet. It still felt like a longshot at best.

And then Williams came alive. He made so many crucial plays down the stretch, so many "did-you-see-that" head-shakers that sometimes his driving basket against Stoudamire with a little less than a minute left is overlooked. But it was perhaps the most signature shot Williams ever made in an Illinois uniform, a bullying basket in which he used his power to pound Stoudamire, to send him spiraling out of the way as he sank the two points that made Allstate Arena really believe.

Suddenly, the unthinkable seemed possible. After Williams' basket, Weber was frantic. Though he can't remember any details, he recalls that he and his coaching staff were in the midst of a frenetic discussion about whether to foul the Wildcats—and if so, whom to hack. But Weber had told his players during a timeout to do what desperate teams always do: Go hard after steals. If you have to foul, don't worry.

Illinois didn't have to foul. Almost before Weber knew what was happening, Williams had poked loose a steal and then, with the basketball almost on his hip, flipped a pinpoint pass ahead to Brown for a layup with 45 seconds to play. Illinois was on a 12-2 run and within three points of Arizona. Allstate Arena was in a frenzy. And hard as you tried, you couldn't hear "Bear Down" coming from anywhere.

The Shot

"The Shot" will be remembered for years, not just by Illinois fans who have worn out tapes of it, but by basketball fans everywhere who saw it. It would be named the "Pontiac Game-Changing Play" of the 2005 NCAA tournament. It would be the seminal moment of Williams' basketball career—perhaps the play, more than any other, that would earn him his ticket into the top three of the NBA draft.

But The Shot was not a one-man show. Jack Ingram had been quietly effective against the Wildcats, had scored eight points and grabbed a few rebounds and done all he could to help try to slow the unstoppable Frye in the post. But Ingram's final major contribution would be one of the biggest defensive plays in Illinois basketball history.

After a timeout, Arizona looked to inbound with a three-point lead, and it appeared as though the game would come down to free throws. But Ingram—perhaps with the aid of a push—found himself within reach of a high inbound pass. He got a hand on the ball. It was all he needed. Williams would corral the tip. Illinois had the ball, and it had time. But Williams wasn't waiting. He stepped into his shot from the right wing and let it fly for the tie. The ball swished, but you couldn't hear it.

Randle and Brock, Illinois' most spectacular dunkers, jumped as high as they ever had in front of the Illini's bench. Bill Murray clutched his chest in disbelief, his eyes rolling skyward. And the Illinois fans at Allstate Arena roared with joy and relief, a sound so loud it was almost quiet, almost swallowed the court in a white noise.

"Definitely the biggest shot of my life," Williams said after the game.

The biggest shot of Arizona's season was certain to come from Stoudamire, and after a timeout, that's where Olson went. But Stoudamire—shockingly—gave the ball up. Instead, Jawann McClellan would shoot the potential game winner. When his shot missed, Stoudamire came up with the long rebound and rose to

"The Shot": Deron Williams' game-tying three pointer completed Illinois'
miraculous comeback against Arizona in the Elite Eight. It will go down as
one of the most memorable baskets in the history of Illinois basketball.
Doug Benc/Getty Images

shoot. He had struggled all night, but these were the moments Stoudamire lived for. The big play. The big shot. The game-winner.

"I was just reaching, doing everything I could to get a piece," Head said.

He did, blocking Stoudamire's attempt. The game was headed to overtime. The fans had turned the inside of Allstate Arena into what sounded like a landing strip at nearby O'Hare.

It Ain't Over 'Til It's Overtime

Williams began overtime as he had ended regulation, burying a three-pointer. But Illinois still hadn't solved Frye, who scored back-to-back baskets to give Arizona the lead back. Powell's driving dunk put the Illini back on top, and though the crowd roared, there was tension underneath that celebration.

Williams and Head turned it to pure joy moments later. Williams would bury yet another three-pointer, strutting back downcourt shaking his head, signaling that he was in the zone. And then Head, still hobbling, stole a pass and raced to the basket for a layup, the sheer determination on his face so evident that Illinois coaches would later turn the image into a T-shirt for their players. The Illini lead was six. As Head turned to go back downcourt, he raised his hand to a celebrating Illinois crowd.

Arizona had one more run left, and Adams led the way. First, he converted a basket and free throw that cut Illinois' lead to three. Then his putback cut the margin to one, and when Head missed a shot with 20 seconds to play, Arizona had one last chance. The Cats called timeout. Williams called for backup.

"I can't guard Stoudamire," Williams told Weber.

Illinois' star was exhausted. He'd given all he had. And everyone in the building knew that the Wildcats would turn to Stoudamire again, despite his miss at the end of regulation. So Head took Stoudamire. Williams was protected. Or so he thought. With Stoudamire struggling—he finished two for 13 from the floor— Olson instead went to the man with the hot hand. The last shot belonged to Adams, who was guarded by the Illini who had just begged off Arizona's clutch shooter, Williams.

Illinois players celebrate after defeating Arizona to advance to the Final Four. *Darrell Hoemann/The News-Gazette*

"I was surprised, but I just had to keep him in front of me," Williams said. "I just didn't want him to get a clean look."

He didn't. Williams contested Adams' two-point jumper, and it slammed off the backboard, not even close, as the horn sounded.

Illinois 90, Arizona 89.

The scoreboard hung from the rafters, plain as day. But it took time to comprehend it. Disbelief couldn't quiet the crowd, which exploded as Illinois players, managers, and coaches piled on top of one another at midcourt.

"The best feeling in the world," McCumber said. "That's my favorite memory from four years."

Williams broke away from the pack to shake hands with the Arizona players, and after he had, Brown ran to his friend and gave him a friendly shove.

"I told you!" Brown said. "I told you!"

Weber, meanwhile, could hardly pull himself together. Earlier in the week, Weber admitted that at times, he still reminded himself to call his mother. He hadn't yet come to terms with her passing. In the wake of his team's miracle comeback, Weber was slammed, blasted with an emotional sledgehammer.

"I was thinking of my mom," he said. "I was thinking of my dad and Coach Keady and all the people who had made sacrifices so that I could get to where I am today. It was a lot to deal with."

Weber, tears streaming down his face, found Gary Nottingham first. They embraced as Weber cried, the din of 14,000 Illinois fans barely loud enough to cover up his sobbing. The tears wouldn't last for long, though. By the time Weber climbed a ladder to clip the remnants of the net, he was wearing a wide smile. He waved the net above his head as fans screamed, "Bruuuuuuuce!"

"This is the most amazing thing I've ever been a part of," Brown said from the middle of a court-turned-moshpit. "I looked in them guys' eyes, my teammates, and I could see they never quit. We believed. We fought. That's why we're going to the Final Four."

12

SEE YOU IN ST. LOUIS

The trip home after even the biggest win goes something like this: Illinois players pile into a bus or plane amped up, riding high on adrenaline. They laugh. They cut up. Then they turn on their CD players and iPods, put on their headphones and fall fast asleep.

After the Illini snapped Wisconsin's homecourt win streak, the flight had been that way. Same for their monster win against Michigan State. The bus ride home from the Arizona game in Chicago, though, had been something altogether different.

"I'm a sleeper," Illinois assistant coach Jay Price said. "I can't remember staying awake for an entire trip home all year. But I never slept on that bus ride. You couldn't. There was too much energy on that bus."

Illinois' charter buses are equipped with VCRs and TV screens, and within minutes after boarding the bus, the players were treated to the last five minutes of regulation and the overtime period of the pulse-pounding game they'd just won. When Jack Ingram's steal led to Deron Williams' game-tying three-pointer, the bus erupted in cheers. And that process repeated.

"We probably watched it five or six times," Williams said. And each time, players shouted when Williams tied the game as if they didn't know it was coming. The moment the game ended, the Illini asked to rewind it again, to the start of the comeback. Then, shortly before Illinois returned to Champaign, the folks closest to the

Dee Brown is all smiles as he gives fans a high-five upon returning to Champaign-Urbana following Illinois' 90-89 victory over Arizona in the Elite Eight. Thousands of fans were waiting for the team's arrival on campus. *Holly Hart/The News-Gazette*

front of the bus spotted a disturbance ahead. Police lights flickered in the distance. Cars appeared to be stopped.

"Somebody was like, 'There must be a *huge* accident up there,'" student manager Matt McCumber said.

It was no accident. On an overpass in Paxton, fans had gathered to cheer the Illini's bus as it passed under on the way home. A police escort led the Illini from there, and at every overpass, it seemed, the same thing was happening. It was midnight, and yet it seemed all of Central Illinois was not only awake, it was ready to party. But the real party was in Champaign. When the team arrived at the Ubben Basketball Complex, thousands of fans waited, cheering wildly as the Illini stepped off the bus.

"The scene was just—it was unbelievable," Weber said. "I think that's when the game really sunk in. That's when you were just [like], 'Wow.'"

For all the affection, Weber felt almost guilty. His players had arrived home in time to join in what was no doubt an equally wild scene on Green Street, the tavern-lined main drag of Champaign's Campustown district. Instead, they would begin their celebration by signing autographs. Countless ones.

"I could have stayed until four in the morning," Weber said. "That's how many people there were. I mean, we had fans around all year, but I had never seen anything like this before."

The players didn't seem to mind.

"It goes to show you that we have the best fans in America," Roger Powell Jr. would say. "And they've been waiting for this."

Showing the Love

It would become clear in the coming days just how much the Illini faithful had been anticipating a return trip to the Final Four. Always a college-basketball-crazed community, Champaign-Urbana went into hoops overdrive in the week leading up to the Final Four. It was impossible to drive down a street without seeing a business with well-wishes on its sign out front. WDWS 1400-AM, the local flagship of the Illini Sports Network, had printed orange Illini signs that fans could post in their front yard, and they were in every neighborhood throughout town. T-shirt stands hawking Illini Final Four merchandise sprung up overnight on countless street corners in town. And local CBS affiliate WCIA was barraged with calls from fans asking when the Arizona game would be re-aired.

"I have a box of cards and letters," Weber said weeks after the season, "that it may take me months to get through."

The Illinois coach wanted his players to soak up the adulation. But not too much. It was rare for Illinois players to have normal days on campus. Autograph requests and photo ops had become part of daily life for the Illini. So Weber figured the sooner he got them away from Champaign, the better.

"I called so many coaches for advice," Weber said. "I wanted to talk to anyone who had been there. I called Jim Calhoun at Connecticut. We put a call in to Georgia Tech. I wanted as much input as I could get on when to get to the site, what we should let them do when they were there."

A New Ballgame

One of Weber's go-to guys for advice was Michigan State's Tom Izzo, who had earned his fourth trip to the Final Four the day after Illinois' win against Arizona by beating Kentucky in an overtime thriller. Weber had watched the game from the basketball offices at Ubben and rooted hard for his friend, at one point tossing an empty water bottle at the television when the Wildcats grabbed an early overtime lead.

If Weber received any consensus from fellow coaches, it was this: Let the players enjoy themselves. Let them stay downtown, close to the action in St. Louis. But rein them in a little as the week goes on, so that by Friday night, they're focused. With that in mind, Weber elected to take his team to St. Louis on Wednesday night, which would allow them all day Thursday to soak up the Final Four.

That Weber sought such advice—that he needed to—was an illustration of one of the biggest storylines from the Final Four. Weber was a rookie on college basketball's biggest stage. The team he would face on Saturday night, Louisville, was guided by a veteran, Rick Pitino, who was taking his third different school to the Final Four. Izzo and North Carolina's Roy Williams, too, were Final Four specialists. But no one in the Illinois camp seemed to worry much about how Weber would handle himself. While he was in St. Louis, he was due to pick up six national coach of the year awards. The inexperience didn't seem to bother anyone.

"If you looked at the rosters of the teams, there was one player who had been to the Final Four, and that was [Michigan State's] Tim Bograkos," Price said. "The last I looked, Coach Weber didn't score any points for us. Coach Pitino didn't score any points, either. It was about the teams."

The Naked Truth

Unlike several of the teams they'd played during the NCAA tournament run, Louisville would be a familiar foe for Illinois. They'd seen the Cardinals play several times during the year, and Dee Brown had become friends during his AAU basketball days with Louisville point guard Taquan Dean. He'd also encountered Pitino in his younger days.

It's an odd story that Brown told me when I first met him, a few days after he'd committed to play for Illinois. The summer before his senior year, Brown had played in an AAU event in Louisville, Kentucky, one of those weekend-long events when players are running frantically all day from game to game. At one point, Brown was forced to change clothes without making a trip to the locker room. He dropped his shorts in the bleachers and began to change.

"I looked over and there's Rick Pitino, just lookin' at me," Brown said. "Not, like, in a weird way, you know. Just kind of, I don't know, looking at me."

Maybe he was just shocked at Brown's boldness: to be able to drop drawers in public. He would soon become personally acquainted with the Illini's boldness on the court, as well.

Do We Have Any Volunteers?

Williams, too, was familiar with the Louisville roster, and the Illinois point guard, who had asked off of Arizona's Salim Stoudamire on the final possession of overtime in the Elite Eight, this time had no qualms about who he wanted to guard. Williams sought out Wayne McClain, the assitant who would scout Louisville.

"I want Garcia," Williams said.

That would be Francisco Garcia, Louisville's small forward and the key to the Cardinals' offense. Though he stood six foot seven, four inches taller than Williams, Garcia wasn't a post-up player. He was more of a point forward, a player who liked the outside jumper and used his dribble to get his teammates involved. "He's really a great player," Weber said. "He really makes them go."

Williams wanted to make him stop. "I like that challenge," Williams said. "I like being able to step up and try to guard the opponent's best guy. You take pride in that."

Warm Sendoff

For Illinois fans, it was about their team getting back to college basketball's promised land, and the Illini faithful wanted to send Illinois off in style. After a Wednesday afternoon practice, the Illini attended a rally at the Assembly Hall that featured the Illini cheerleaders, the school band, and thousands of Illinois fans. The Hall had been set up for a home and garden show that weekend, so the court Illinois had dominated during the regular season was stowed in storage. The Illini still looked right at home, though, entering to squealing fans at the end of the rally.

Before the Illini arrived, several Illinois coaches had taken the microphone to warm up the crowd, notably football coach Ron Zook, who had been hired in December to replace the fired Ron Turner. Zook, who had been fired at Florida, came to Illinois with a reputation as a master recruiter, and he'd wisely affiliated himself with the most popular sport on campus. He donned an orange sweater for home games, had attended the Arizona game in Rosemont and brought cheers at the rally when he gave fans a line he'd used several times before: "We've got to take all this orange in here and take it across the street," he said, referring to Memorial Stadium, Illinois' football home.

But while Zook had gotten the crowd started, it was the arrival of the Illini that whipped it into a frenzy. Weber spoke to the crowd first, to thank fans for their support, to promise that the Illini would give their all in the quest to bring back the big trophy. The most boisterous moment, though, came courtesy of the team's spokesman, Jack Ingram. After thanking the Illini fans on behalf of the team, Ingram said, "We're going to go down to St. Louis and get rid of that label 'Best program to never win the national championship!'"

The crowd roared, and the Illini left to the blaring of the school's fight song by the Illini pep band. The cheering of fans echoed through the Hall long after Illinois players had walked down a tunnel and boarded their bus. The bus ride to St. Louis was mostly uneventful, until the Illini got within close range of the Final Four host city. Weber had driven into town countless times as a head coach, both at Southern Illinois and Illinois. He admitted, though, that he'd never seen St. Louis quite the way he did that night. It seemed more alive, somehow, the living, breathing culmination of a goal, those cityscape pictures from the Illinois locker room finally brought to life.

"I went over that bridge probably 200 times or more," Weber said. "But that night it was different. It was a clear, beautiful night, the Arch was all lit up. Coming into the city, it really meant something. That's when it hit you: 'We're in the Final Four.'"

Weber was having a moment. And true to form, his players turned it into a laugh riot.

"Hey Coach, would you duck down?" Deron Williams called out from the back of the bus. "Your head's blockin' the Arch."

Final Focus

Part of Weber's plan to get the Illini out of Champaign early had been to avoid distraction, and for the most part it had worked. Players had limited access to tickets, and their friends and family knew it. So ticket requests—for the players, if not for Weber—were relatively few. And though the sheer number of media at the Final Four was unlike anything even the Illini had experienced all year, the interview sessions were regimented and limited to about an hour. So Weber could let his players focus on Louisville. Still, he told them not to do so at the expense of having some fun.

"There's got to be a point when you come out on the court where you just stop," Weber said. "Smell the roses. Whatever. Take it all in. Get the snapshot. Realize what you've accomplished."

All season, the Final Four had been Illinois' goal. With that goal checked off, Weber now wanted his team focused on winning the national championship. But he also wanted his players to have some fun.

"I think in a lot of ways, the pressure was in getting there," Williams said. "Once we got there, I think we did relax. I think we were loose. We were having fun."

Red with Envy

The Illini had an uneventful Thursday of Final Four week. Weber had intended for his players to get a chance to soak up some of the St. Louis atmosphere, but that became problematic. Illinois had its own personal security guard, a Champaign police officer who'd been traveling with the team since midseason, and he could discourage some autograph-seekers when the Illini traveled in a pack. But if Illinois players wanted to break off in small groups and explore, say, the Landing, the bar and restaurant district not far from the Edward Jones Dome?

"Pretty much impossible," McCumber said. "They'd get swarmed."

So the Illini lay low, eating team meals and practicing but keeping public appearances to a minimum until Friday's open shootaround, which in itself was a staggering event. Illinois fans descended on the Edward Jones Dome in such huge numbers that the three other teams in the field were left somewhat dumbfounded. Louisville, in particular, seemed shocked that the team they would be playing on Saturday apparently had so many more fans in town.

Earlier in the week, Pitino had joked that Louisville had drawn its mascot name—the Cardinals—from "that great baseball team they have there in St. Louis." It was Pitino's way of acknowledging what most fans suspected, that the Cardinals' fans would be wildly outnumbered in St. Louis. But apparently even that hadn't prepared the Cards for the onslaught of orange at the shootaround—a display one Louisville player equated to "being in a carton of Tropicana."

"I got a little worried when I walked out there, because I didn't see any Cardinal fans," Louisville senior Ellis Myles said. "But they'll be here. It's only Friday. Our fans have to work, man. They have jobs."

The Illini fans, though, were putting in work for their team. And it wasn't going unnoticed.

"Everybody had told us that there will come a moment, sometime during the week, when it's going to hit your kids and they'll be like, 'Okay, we're at the Final Four,'" Price said. "For us, I think that was the moment. We ran out for the shootaround and there were all those fans in orange, and that's when it sunk in for the kids. It was exciting. And I don't know if our fans realized how much that meant to our guys. I say this honestly—our fans might have gotten us through to Monday night. They meant that much."

Gucci and the Good Ol' Boy

On the surface, Pitino and Weber couldn't have been more different. Weber had once been the target of ridicule for his wardrobe—*from his own fans*—while Pitino favored tailored suits and Gucci loafers. Pitino owned horses. He had a stake in a restaurant. Weber owned an orange sportcoat and, as coaches go, was blue-collar.

Pitino had coached Kentucky and the Boston Celtics. Weber came to Illinois from Carbondale. And yet, their teams could scarcely have been more similar. The backcourt players were the stars. The three-point shot was a weapon of choice. Even their hearts beat to the same unstoppable rhythm. On the very day Illinois rallied from 15 down to beat Arizona, Louisville—trailing by 18 points in the first half—had stormed back from the brink of defeat against West Virginia.

And both teams had brought once-proud programs back to the Final Four and were basking in the gratitude. Days before the Final Four, James Augustine had a conversation at a bowling alley with an elderly woman who wanted to talk about nothing but the Final Four.

"For all those people who have lived in Champaign for years and years, it's kind of fun to bring the pride back," Augustine said.

Louisville felt much the same way. "All year we had fans telling us, 'Please take us back to the Final Four. We want to be there. We want to see how it feels,'" Garcia said.

They were about to find out. Both teams had made a long climb back—Illinois to its first Final Four since 1989, Louisville to its first since 1986—but only one was advancing to Monday. They played a whole game that Saturday night to determine which it would be. But one play told the whole story.

The Reverend Preys on Pitino

Louisville had been one of the nation's hottest teams down the stretch, and there was no reason to believe that the Cardinals wouldn't put up a fight against the Illini. The two teams were mirror images—talented, experienced and gutsy—and for the first half, they played that way. Illinois led 31-28 at halftime, and each team had its moments. But it became clear early on in the second half that the Illini were in a class ahead of the Cardinals. And nobody illustrated the gap more that Roger Powell Jr., the revved-up Reverend who played like a man possessed in the second half.

Louisville claimed its first—and only—lead of the game early in the half at 34-33, but then Powell took over. With the shot clock winding down, he drained a three-pointer from the top of the key. On the next trip downcourt, he launched another. But where the first had felt true, Powell's second attempt seemed off. As soon as it left his hand, he knew it wasn't going in, so he just went after it. Powell rebounded his own missed three-pointer and slammed the ball through the rim, a ferocious two-handed dunk that became the signature highlight of his senior season. He raised his arms to the sky, pointing to the heavens, as he got back on defense.

"That was a huge lift," Brown said, and though Louisville would tie the game, then claw to within a point later in the second half, Illinois stayed in control. Powell finished with 20 points—18 in the second half—and Head made four second-half three-pointers as the Illini pulled away to a 72-57 win. Williams also lived up to the challenge he'd taken on against Garcia, holding Louisville's star to two-for-10 shooting.

"They truly are a great team," Pitino said. "I don't know if they had the most talent I've seen from a Final Four [team], but they're the best team I've seen in some time."

Roger Powell Jr. celebrates after slamming home the rebound of his own missed three-pointer against Louisville. Powell and Luther Head tied for the team lead in scoring with 20 points. *John Dixon/The News-Gazette*

That team had one last challenge, against the winner of North Carolina-Michigan State, which would tip off later that night. Weeks before Illinois' Senior Night win against Purdue, Weber had written the date of the game—March 3—on the dry erase board in Illinois' locker room. That, he said, was the date the Illini could clinch the Big Ten. After the game, Weber had written a new date on the board: April 4, the date of the NCAA title game.

"Hopefully," Augustine said, "we've got one more step."

13

BITTERSWEET ENDING

College basketball had been clamoring all season for an Illinois-North Carolina final, fans and media practically begging the two to get together in April for a meeting that would answer the question that had been hanging over college hoops since December: who was the better team? The game got what it wanted—maybe what it needed—when North Carolina beat Michigan State 87-71. Illinois fans had been pulling hard for their Big Ten brethren, organizing a T-shirt exchange in which Illini fans brought an extra orange shirt and Michigan State fans an extra green one so that the fans could dress accordingly in pulling for their friendly rivals.

The college game had been enjoying a Renaissance season. *Sports Illustrated* had written about the sport's return in a midseason story, and TV ratings were up across the board. It had been a banner year for the sport. It seemed only fitting that the two best teams—the two teams that had dominated most of the regular season—would play for the biggest banner. It seemed almost like destiny. And yet, with so much time to prepare, some reporters clearly hadn't put much thought into the game. Hence, the public was given the oversimplified blurb that would come to sum up the NCAA championship game: "Talent vs. Team."

It was, from the start, a ridiculous moniker, one that sold short both North Carolina and Illinois. The Tar Heels, the "Talent" in that equation, were painted as a sort of team getting by on sheer athletic ability. And Illinois, the "Team," started two first-round draft picks in its backcourt and had reached the Final Four thanks to far more than its passing. The simplification didn't sit well with either side.

"If that's what people want to say, that's fine," Dee Brown said. "But I think we've got a lot of talent on this team."

"That kind of makes me mad that they would say that," said Sean May of North Carolina. "I know this is a team. We didn't get to this point just by being talented."

But that was the story. Carolina was NBA-ready. Illinois was something out of *Hoosiers*. And the Illini, in the eyes of most of the nation's analysts, were the favorites to win. Finally! The respect Illinois had sought so long was flowing free in the wake of the March the Illini had endured. Winning the Big Ten tournament after Bruce Weber's personal tragedy, rallying in miracle fashion against Arizona, blitzing a powerful Louisville team: all of it had created a sense that Illinois was somehow destined to claim its first-ever national championship. The Illini would erase—as Jack Ingram had promised at the pre-Final Four pep rally—the stigma of being the best program without an NCAA title.

Carolina had a better collection of players. Illinois had the better team. That was the story in an oversimplified nutshell. Not that the players much cared.

"Let's just play the game," Brown said. "Real recognize real. Them dudes have a great team. We have a great team. Let's play and sort it out."

A Day (Un)Like Any Other

It would make a compelling story to say that Illinois was on pins and needles on Sunday, the day between its semifinal win against Louisville and the national championship game. But it would be a lie. Despite the stakes, it was just another day for Illinois. There were media responsibilities, and the Illini handled them without complaint, the players coming across in their breakout interviews— unlike in Rosemont, these were in actual rooms, with doors—as funny and likable. The season had worn on them, but win or lose, the days of constant media attention were about to end. Maybe the Illini were getting nostalgic.

Deron Williams filled notebooks when he told reporters that, as a kid, he'd dreamed of cutting down the nets at the Final Four—as a Carolina Tar Heel. That sort of story is what Final Four Sunday is all about. The questions players get (and the answers they give) are reflective. It's about the game, of course, but it's about the journey, too. It's about who these teams are who've reached college basketball's pinnacle.

It was an opportunity for reflection. I thought of Dee Brown, waiting for his first meeting with Weber after he'd been hired to replace Self, telling me as we leaned against the upstairs railing at the Ubben Basketball Complex, "I'd transfer right now if I could." I thought of Head's journey to this championship game, through his ups and downs. I thought of Weber's frustration early in his first season, when his players questioned the need for his conditioning drills and doubted his motion offense. "That was just us being babies," Williams said.

In a year, they'd grown into men. And Weber knew that his grown-up players would be moving on. Luther Head, Roger Powell Jr., Jack Ingram, Nick Smith, and walk-on Fred Nkemdi were seniors. Williams had told his teammates early in the season that he'd likely declare for the NBA draft after his junior season, but his brilliant tournament run had taken that from a probability to a foregone conclusion. Brown, too, figured at least to flirt with the NBA.

"I know you don't have this opportunity, this group of kids [often]," Weber said. "You know, there is a sense of urgency to it. I've enjoyed the ride. We've had a great journey. It's just been so much fun from Day 1 this season. We're just hoping to finish the storybook season with a great ending."

That night, away from the TV camera lights and tape recorders, Illinois had its customary team meeting. It was the same before every game, a few last-minute details, a chance for coaches and players to get on the same page on the eve of a game. All day, players and coaches had behaved as they always did. The players laughed and joked—if they hadn't, Weber would've worried—and played video games in their hotel rooms. But the mood changed at that night's meeting.

"That was, honestly, probably the saddest part of the whole weekend," Illinois assistant Jay Price said. "Just looking around the room, knowing that whatever happened against Carolina, it was the last time this group would be together this way, the last time that family would all be together, it was really emotional."

Beginning of the End

For the college basketball purist, the modern version of Final Four Saturday is perhaps the best day of the year. It features all the key ingredients in what makes college basketball so enticing to follow: two games, four great teams, the losers go home with no consolation prize. But championship night has a unique energy that Saturday—for all its thrills—can't match, particularly on site. It's the most-watched college basketball game of every season. It's the winner-take-all moment that separates the game from college football and makes it special. And there's a buzz that only that kind of stage can create.

As Illinois and North Carolina warmed up, if they felt that buzz, they hid it well. Each team looked cool and collected. Illinois had a huge advantage in the stands, but on the court, it was clear that the Tar Heels were unlike anything the Illini had seen. Even Arizona, with its stockpile of pro-caliber players, didn't compare to the Tar Heels, who had the swagger of a team full of NBA-ready talent.

Illinois, too, looked ready. The Illini had been waiting for this game their whole lives. They'd been waiting for this opponent all season. But Carolina had been waiting, too. And in the first half, the Heels were the ones who looked hungry.

Early on, it was Rashad McCants—the poster child for North Carolina's supposed me-first dysfunction—who put his stamp on the game. He had 14 points by halftime, but the Tar Heels, contrary to their reputation, were blitzing Illinois as a team. Sean May was unstoppable inside, and it didn't help that Augustine was in foul

Jack Ingram attempts to guard Tar Heel Sean May, who scored 26 points and grabbed 10 rebounds in North Carolina's 75-70 win over Illinois.
John Dixon/The News-Gazette

trouble. May overpowered the Illini, and though Illinois fans were calling for charges against the Tar Heel center, they never came.

By halftime, Carolina led 40-27. Illinois was in a deep hole against a supremely talented team. They'd been there before, against Arizona. And this deficit, despite coming so much earlier, felt eerily similar. The Tar Heels were scoring with ease. And every basket Illinois got seemed to be a chore.

As always, the Illini sat alone in the locker room for the first five minutes of halftime while the coaching staff met to discuss second-half adjustments. For a while, no one spoke. Then Williams and Jack Ingram chimed in.

"We've got one more shot," Williams told his teammates. "We can't go out like this. We got 20 minutes to get back in this and win the national championship."

Weber's message was similar. All season long, his team had shown amazing resilience when the stakes were high: at home and on the road against Iowa; in crunch time at Michigan; at Wisconsin, staring down the barrel of an unbeatable streak; through the emotions of the Big Ten tournament week; and against insurmountable odds against Arizona.

"If you're going to go down," Weber told his team, "you go down fighting."

Battling Back

The Illini, it turned out, had a little more fight left. As May continued to control the paint, Illinois fought back with its most dangerous offensive weapon, the three-point shot. The Illini made seven in the second half, and even as Carolina threatened to run away, those long shots and Illinois' increasingly stingy defense got Weber's team back into the game.

Augustine still couldn't avoid foul trouble ("He felt like he never got in the game," Weber would say later), and he played only nine minutes total before fouling out. But Ingram fought May and made the Tar Heels work defensively, scoring 11 points and grabbing seven rebounds. His presence stretched the Heels' defense, and lanes to the basket were open, the better to create open three-point looks.

When Head buried Illinois' seventh three-pointer of the half with 2:40 to play, Illinois had—against all odds—completed its comeback. The Illini had tied the game. And the momentum of the game seemed to have changed. The theory was that the Illini had been made of sterner stuff than the Heels, that if the game was close down the stretch, Illinois had an edge. But again, Carolina disproved convention.

Deron Williams missed an open three-pointer with 2:03 to play that would've given the Illini the lead. Instead, Marvin Williams put the Heels back on top with a tip-in. Twenty-one seconds later, a wide-open Head launched from three-point range. It was the kind of shot he'd made all season. But he missed. Ingram rebounded Head's miss, and Illinois came out of a timeout with the chance—

In his bright orange blazer, Bruce Weber pleads with the referees during the NCAA championship game. Jack Ingram and James Augustine, who were given the job of trying to guard North Carolina center Sean May, were whistled for nine fouls in the game. May, meanwhile, was called for just one. *John Dixon/The News-Gazette*

again—to tie or take the lead. Williams missed again from three-point range. Again, the look was clean.

"Those are exactly the shots we want," Weber said. "That's the kind of shot we took all year. Usually they go in. If you're looking at shots to win the game, those are the shots you'd want."

But for all the misses, Illinois still had a chance. Powell had rebounded Williams' last misfire, and the Illini—yet again—had an opportunity. But Head tried to penetrate and throw a pass back out onto the perimeter, and Carolina's Raymond Felton saw it coming. Felton picked off the pass—only Illinois' eighth turnover of the game—and free throws would seal the game from there. Head, who finished the game with a team-high 21 points, missed two more three-pointers in the closing minutes. As the final horn sounded and confetti erupted from the rafters at the Edward Jones Dome, he hung his head.

McCants—who hadn't scored in the second half—raised the "North Carolina" in his jersey, a sure sign of just how much Brown's trademark move had permeated the college scene. And May pumped his fist toward the Carolina faithful. He'd celebrated his 21st birthday with 26 points, the exact total his father Scott had scored in leading Indiana to the 1976 NCAA championship.

In its own way, the end was as surreal as the Arizona scene had been. Deron Williams tried to shake hands with the Tar Heels, as he had with the Wildcats. Weber walked off the court, his eyes dry but his expression stunned. The shots were supposed to fall. It wasn't supposed to end this way—not in Year 100, the most endearing of them all.

In the Aftermath

As with every game, there was a cooling-off period in the Illinois locker room, and the Illini, heartbroken and teary-eyed, needed it to compose themselves. Particularly inconsolable was Head, whose uncharacteristic turnover had been crucial. The senior who had played his last game in orange and blue, who had nailed five three-pointers and given all he had, apologized to his teammates. He told

Members of the media surround a saddened Dee Brown in the locker room following Illinois' loss in the championship game. *AP/WWP*

them he was sorry for costing them the game. No one was accepting.

"Luther," Weber said, "you're the reason why we're here."

Brian Randle, the redshirt sophomore who hadn't played a minute all season, who only recently had rejoined practices after having his left hand surgically repaired, wrapped an arm around Head's shoulder.

"Out of everybody since I got here, you're the one I look up to the most," Randle said.

The tears had all been shed by the time reporters filed into the locker room. Players sunk into the benches in their lockers, and did their best to answer questions about what had happened and about what lay ahead. Yes, Williams admitted, he would take a close look at the NBA. Brown bristled at the question, but said he'd discuss it later. In perhaps the strangest of the postgame scenes, Brown, finished with his interviews, slumped into a chair in front of his locker and stared into space as a dozen photographers snapped away, capturing what was the definitive image of Illinois' postgame pain.

Brown's expression never changed. Unchanged, too, was Weber. Even in the wake of the most painful defeat of his career, he was, as always, the everyman, the staggeringly normal coach of the nation's second-best team. When a television cameraman slid off the chair he'd perched himself on to film Weber in the locker room surrounded by reporters, his camera hit me square in the face, just under the eye. Weber hardly missed a beat.

"You okay?" he asked. Assured that I was, he returned to fielding questions.

"How can you be sad?" Weber said. "If you're sad, you're sad that the journey's over, not about this game. We played a great team. We gave a great effort. We went down fighting. I'm not saying I didn't want to win the game. But if you're sad about this, I feel sorry for you. It doesn't get any better than this."

It was a sentiment his players, bleary-eyed and hoarse, did their best to echo.

"Of course I'm sad—I'm sad that it's over, that we lost," Williams said. "But we did great things this year. We got to the Final Four. We played for the national championship. Maybe some people who weren't too excited about Illinois basketball are excited now."

A Heroes' Welcome

The bus ride home the following afternoon was unsurprisingly somber. Along the way, coaches and players wondered what awaited them in Champaign. A celebration had been planned for Memorial Stadium late that afternoon, but it had been set before the game, a win or lose proposition. In the wake of the loss, the Illinois staff didn't know what to expect.

"We literally were wondering if anybody would show up," Price said. "This honestly was the discussion we had: 'Do you think anybody will be there?' We didn't know if our fans would be there."

Oh, they were there—20,000 of them. That's 4,000 more than the number who showed up in Chapel Hill, North Carolina, to welcome the national champions.

Deron Williams and Bruce Weber share a moment together during a celebration held at Memorial Stadium following the team's return to campus after their loss in the title game. Approximately 20,000 fans were in attendance. *AP/WWP*

"Any sadness you had, this kind of takes it away," Weber said. "The sun did come up, and the orange came out."

Players filed off the team bus as they were introduced, and the planned program featured several speeches, including words from Weber, athletic director Ron Guenther, a few players, and even Illinois Gov. Rod Blagojevich, who was booed by many fans, drawing a chuckle from Weber. But the celebration's most poignant moment had no words. After the player introductions, Brown, Head, and Williams—the players who'd come to symbolize Illinois' season—gathered together and embraced. The gesture had a finality to it, a sense of goodbye. What had begun on that chilly October day had ended against North Carolina, but it didn't feel that way until that moment.

Williams would enter the NBA draft after all, signing with an agent and ultimately being drafted third overall by the Utah Jazz. Head, brilliant in the league's Chicago predraft camp, found his way into the first round, too, selected 24th overall by the Houston Rockets. Meanwhile, seniors Powell and Ingram—who went undrafted—would battle it out in the NBA's summer league, in the hopes of impressing a coach or general manager enough to get their shot at the NBA.

The Utah Jazz traded up three spots in the draft in order to be able to select Williams. He was the first point guard selected in the 2005 draft, and the highest selection in the history of Illinois basketball. A multimillion-dollar NBA contract awaited him.

Brown, too, entered the draft after his junior year. But he didn't sign with an agent, and after breaking his foot in the predraft camp, he announced his plans to return for his senior season. He was excited at the news conference announcing his decision, but he was philosophical, too. Things would change in his senior year. He'd been one of three, and though he was excited about a new, expanded leadership role, about helping Augustine form the core of a new team, there was sadness, too.

"Playing with Luther and Deron was amazing," Brown said. "I was a different player around those dudes. My game was more amazing than ever. But things change. We had to break it up eventually."

The Season Lingers On

Sometimes when Price is jogging he still thinks about those shots, the open ones that wouldn't fall in the title game. He wonders what might've happened if... .

Sometimes when Weber is out on a recruiting trip or at a public speaking engagement, he's reminded just how much the season meant to Illinois fans. Walking down the street in Chicago one day in the spring, he heard someone yell his name only to see a city bus driver who'd stopped his bus on the street to shout his thanks to his favorite coach.

Sometimes when Luther Head is alone in his room, he reflects back on his last year of college, of the times he had with Brown and Williams and the rest of his teammates, of road trips and big shots and the wild ride he says he wouldn't trade for the world.

"If I could've left early [for the NBA], I don't think I would have," Head said. "That's how much I loved this school and those guys."

It's the kind of year, all three would agree, that you never forget. It might be the kind you never repeat.

"I'm not crazy," Weber said. "I know I might coach the rest of my life and never have another year like that. But that doesn't mean I can't try."

ACKNOWLEDGMENTS

Writing a book sounds like a one-man proposition. I thought so right up until I wrote this, my first one. Turns out, it takes a lot of people to do one of these things. I'm glad to get the chance to thank them.

First and foremost, I thank the 2004-05 Illini, whose professionalism and candor made covering the team—and by extension, writing this book—much easier. Special thanks go to Dee Brown, Deron Williams, and Luther Head. This is the story of a team, but those three were its heart, and their patience throughout the year is greatly appreciated.

I couldn't have done this without the season-long cooperation of Bruce Weber and his coaching and support staff: Wayne McClain, Jay Price, Tracy Webster, Gary Nottingham, Rod Cardinal, Al Martindale, Cindy Butkovich, and a crew of managers, especially Matt McCumber. It also didn't hurt that Illinois has two of the best sports information directors on earth in Kent Brown and Derrick Burson.

Like writing a book, covering a beat is a team effort, and the entire sports staff at *The News-Gazette* played a role in this. I'd be remiss if I didn't thank the following for their help along the way: Jeff Huth, Fred Kroner, Rich Barak, Tony Mancuso, Mike Goebel, Mike Colgan, Brian Dietz, Bob Asmussen, Tony Bleill, and especially Jeff Mezydlo, my friend and road warrior.

I'd never have learned to navigate Illinois basketball, nor the Big Ten, without the assistance of Loren Tate, the best and most patient tour guide I can imagine. And I'd never have been given the opportunity if not for Jim Rossow, a good friend and the best sports editor on the planet.

I don't say thanks often enough to my parents, Lonnie and Sharon Dawson, or my brother Brian, for their support. Nor to Pat

Forde, Chuck Culpepper, and Rusty Hampton—three of the best mentors and friends a sportswriter could have—for their guidance and friendship.

Covering the 2004-05 season was a nonstop rollercoaster ride, made more fun by the friends in and out of the media who shared it with me: Lindsey Willhite, Travis Drury, Bobby LaGesse, Ian Gold, Lisa Koulias, Courtney Linehan, Jeremy Rutherford, Ben Taylor, and John Brumbaugh, among the many.

Finally, it took a bunch of friends to keep me distracted and (mostly) sane when I needed to talk about something—anything— besides the motion offense and the Big Ten race. For that, I thank Alison Kight, Ben Boldt, Will Messer, Steve Jones, Matt May, Travis Hubbard, Jeb Messer, Alex Williams, Jordan Phelps, Brad Taylor, Dwayn Chambers, Colin Casebolt, Dustin Stamper, and all the rest of my Kentucky surfers.